For Maggie,

from

Michael

10.6.82

HEIRS AND GRACES

Heirs & Graces

The Claim to the Dukedom of Leinster

Michael Estorick

WEIDENFELD AND NICOLSON
LONDON

Published in Great Britain by
Weidenfeld and Nicolson Ltd
91 Clapham High Street
London sw4 7TA

ISBN 0 297 77955 9

Set, printed and bound in Great Britain by
Fakenham Press Limited, Fakenham, Norfolk

AUTHOR'S NOTE

*It is hereby acknowledged that any inferences, opinions, and conclu-
sions expressed in this book are based on my own interpretation of the
facts.*

For Isobel

Contents

Acknowledgements

IT would be untrue to say that this book is all our own work; it would not have been possible without the co-operation, advice and support of a large number of people. To the following we owe a special debt: the Duke and Duchess of Leinster, the Dowager Duchess of Leinster, Brigadier Denis FitzGerald, Patricia Roberts, Glen S. Roberts, Leonard FitzGerald, Theresa Caudhill, S. Cupples Scudder, Edward Pierce, the Bennett sisters, Reginald Tyler and George Tyler.

We would also like to express our gratitude to James Fitz-Gerald, William Synott, the late Sir Fergus Graham, Lady Graham, Sir Martyn Beckett, the late Sir George Mallaby, Patrick Montague-Smith, Anita Leslie, Leonard Watts, Leslie Dodson, Dr Patrick Strong, Marigold Phillips and her mother, the late Mrs Charrington. Thanks are also due to Colonel Nixon of the King's Royal Rifles, the staff of the Imperial War Museum and the Irish Guards Headquarters; the Royal Archivist, Windsor; Kneller Hall; the late Hans Tasiemka and the staff of the Tasiemka Library; Cheam School; Michael Davie, Ian Davie, James Thompson, Powerscreen International (owners of Carton), Ann, Countess of Feversham, Prunella Bathurst-Norman, Mrs Foster, Ivan Sharp, Nin Dunham, the late Jimmy Brown, Alan Stewart, Henry Morgenstern, Dr Gordon Prince, the office of the *News of the World*; to Hugh Popham, Carol Illingworth, Geyla Frank, Candia Howard and Emily Nomer for their work on the manuscript; to Sydney Gruson of the *New York Times* and Michael and Dorothy Blankfort; to our agent Michael Thomas and editor Marcia Fenwick; and to Robert Jarman for suggesting the book in the first place.

Finally, we owe a deep debt of gratitude to Tom McGuire, David Vineyard, Colonel John Moloney, and Arthur and Charlie Jamieson for their friendship and for their research, on which much of the text is based.

Michael Estonick
John Ford
London 1981

Illustrations

Prologue

CRAIGHOUSE is an imposing building in a suburb of Edinburgh, standing high on a hill overlooking the Firth of Forth. By day it is forbidding; by night it is frankly ominous, with its long and intricate neo-Gothic façade, its helmet-shaped cupolas, its high rectangular chimney-stacks and row upon row of narrow, barred windows. Its function is unmistakable: Craighouse is an asylum for the insane.

A short distance from the main building, but still within its grounds, there were once a number of apartments reserved for the more socially respectable lunatics. Here the supervision was relatively unobtrusive, though medical attention and burly keepers were within reach, and, for those with the correct credentials, some semblance – albeit a travesty – of another life could be recreated. It was here, at the Bungalow, 153 Morningside Drive that, according to the hospital records, a man known to his fellow inmates as Mr FitzGerald died ten minutes after midnight on the morning of 2 February 1922.

Within a few hours Fergus Graham, then in his late twenties, was notified of his cousin's death and hurried north. In Carlisle he met Dr Pollock, the deceased's personal physician. Together the two men escorted the coffin across the Irish Sea for burial. More than forty years later both men still vividly remembered the terrible crossing by steamer from Stranraer.

When the boat docked at Dublin, the coffin was transferred to a hearse which carried it the fourteen miles to Maynooth, on the border of Carton, the deceased's vast estate. Family retainers carried the coffin from the gates to the small family graveyard, where the man was laid to rest beside his mother and father, his paternal grandparents, and other less immediate kin.

A few years earlier Mr FitzGerald's funeral would have been accorded considerable attention by press and public, would indeed have been something of a national event. Now not even the local newspaper printed an announcement.

Since 1916 the British had been fighting the Irish insurgents, and from 1919 warfare had ravaged the country. However, by the end of 1921 the violence had abated; a peace treaty was signed with Lloyd George's government in London which, after much deliberation and heartache had been ratified by the Irish Parliament. For many this treaty was nothing short of a sell-out, ratification a source of national shame. Far from restoring peace, it only divided the country even further; within weeks the destruction of lives and property began again. Houses were burned, property vandalized, men and women executed in an orgy of reprisal which has continued to this day. Partition was already an established fact in 1922.

But if more momentous events were taking place, capturing public interest in a way a private funeral never could, it was still a surprisingly quiet event. For the family of the deceased, few of whom bothered to attend, wanted it so – and not for reasons associated with the political and social upheaval fomenting around them. Because of their unique place in Irish history and society the family of 'Mr FitzGerald' would be spared the effects of the coming civil war, but for them his death was as great a cataclysm as any assassin's bullet.

Prologue

When the gravestone, a large flat Celtic cross, was laid, its inscription was simple. It consisted only of the words: 'In Loving Memory of Maurice Duke of Leinster Died February 2nd 1922 Aged 35'. Of all the gravestones in the cemetery at Carton it was the only one to omit a date of birth.

He must have been born on 1 March, for on that day in 1908 the countryside had celebrated his coming of age with a bonfire and barrels of beer. A torchlight procession preceding two marching bands had wound through Maynooth, and the young Duke was presented with an illuminated address. Some said he had lit the bonfire himself, others did not remember his having attended the festivities at all. In the merrymaking the young man had perhaps passed unnoticed. But, if his coming of age had been in March 1908, surely he would have been thirty-four and not thirty-five at the time of his death?

Now that he was dead, those standing about the grave endeavoured to remember what they could of him: it was not much. The coffin was laid to rest, and the congregation dispersed quickly. But, before they departed, the pallbearers debated hotly among themselves; long after the occasion they were remembered as saying the coffin was far too light to have contained the body of a man.

Almost half a century after the funeral a small obituary notice appeared in the *San Francisco Chronicle*. A man named Maurice Francis FitzGerald had died the previous day, 13 November 1967, at the age of eighty. Born in Ireland, he had been educated at Eton and a military school in Scotland. In 1908 he had left Ireland for Canada. Arriving in California in 1913 he had worked as a rough rider in wild west shows and had travelled widely. During the First World War he had served in the Canadian Forces. In the early 1930s he had taken bit parts in movies; later he had became a rancher in St Louis. For the last

3

fifteen years of his life he had lived quietly in retirement in Marin County, north of San Francisco. He was survived by a widow, a brother, three children and eight grandchildren.

But what probably aroused most interest among the paper's readers was that Maurice FitzGerald was described as having been the sixth Duke of Leinster. 'Fitz-Gerald', the *San Francisco Chronicle* wrote, 'declared himself legally dead in 1922 in order for the title to pass to his brother, Lord Edward Fitz-Gerald of Sussex, England, who is the 7th Duke.'

On 8 March 1976, in a small London flat, a white-haired old man was found in a state of semi-consciousness by his wife. Shortly afterwards he died in the ambulance taking him to hospital. His last recorded words were, 'Oh, for the peace of Ford Manor.' Ford Manor, near Lingfield in Surrey, was his former home.

The old man was Edward FitzGerald, described the following day in the *Daily Express* as 'Four times a bridegroom, three times a bankrupt, jet setter in the days before jets, boutique owner, knitwear designer, transatlantic sailor, long-distance walker'. He was also since 1922 Baron and Earl of Offaly, Baron Kildare of Kildare, Viscount Leinster of Taplow, Earl and Marquess of Kildare and seventh Duke of Leinster, the premier nobleman of Ireland.

Five months later the office of the *News of the World* in London received a telex from San Francisco. A Californian school-teacher named Leonard FitzGerald was laying claim to the dukedom of Leinster, made vacant in March of that year by the death of the seventh Duke. According to Leonard, his father, Maurice Francis FitzGerald, had been the seventh Duke's predecessor; as a young man he had escaped from his family to America and had later 'abdicated' in favour of his younger brother Edward. As it was not legally possible for a title to be

4

transferred a false declaration of his death had been made in Edinburgh in 1922. This claim was far from straightforward; the story unfolded in the lengthy telex revealed anomalies and complications that were to start an investigation into a mystery as peculiar as any which has marked the long history of the British peerage.

1

From Castle to Council Flat

THERE is still something awe-inspiring about a duke, the highest-ranking, although not the oldest, title in the peerage. Non-royal dukedoms were granted for a variety of reasons, but when the twentieth Earl of Kildare was created Duke of Leinster in 1766 it was simply in recognition of his family's pre-eminence in Irish history. The Earl had previously been granted an English viscountcy – entitling him to a seat in the House of Lords – on his marriage to a duke's daughter in 1747; he had built the stateliest town house in Dublin (it now houses the Irish Parliament); he was a Privy Councillor, a Lieutenant-General and the Governor of County Kildare. He was the most popular peer in Ireland. After some six centuries of devoted service to Ireland it was fitting that the FitzGeralds should be granted the first dukedom in the Irish peerage (the only other Irish dukedom is that of Abercorn, created in 1868).

The FitzGeralds, or Geraldines, had come to Ireland in the twelfth century, after the Norman invasion. Barons of Offaly since 1205, the first Earl of Kildare was created in 1316. For more than three hundred years they ruled like princes over the fertile land of County Kildare, intermarrying with the Irish, and adopting their language, manners and customs; they fought ceaselessly, with great effect. It was one of the great soldier-statesman Earls of Kildare who introduced the gun to Ireland. They also founded the great Franciscan and Dominican monasteries in the country, and amassed an enviable library of early Irish manuscripts and printed books. The almost total power of the FitzGeralds in the sixteenth century was finally crushed by Henry VIII, to whom the castle of Maynooth fell. Thereafter they lived the lives of country gentlemen, albeit on a very grand scale, and took little interest in politics.

In 1739 the family moved to Carton, a fine but old-fashioned house. The nineteenth Earl of Kildare instructed Richard Castle, the prominent Irish architect, to convert and extend the existing house, which he did by lengthening the body of the house by two bays, raising it by one storey and connecting it by curved colonnades to wings containing stables and kitchens. It was magnificent when completed; the alterations cost the Earl £21,000. Sadly, he did not enjoy his palatial residence for long, his son – who later became the first Duke – succeeding him in 1744. The first Duke's wife, Lady Emily Lennox, occupied herself with de-formalizing the garden and creating an extensive park with a cunningly contrived series of lakes in the 'natural' style made famous by Capability Brown.

The second Duke also centred his life round Carton and was largely responsible for the design of the new town of Maynooth and for improving methods of farming on his estate. He entertained lavishly, and on a visit there in 1778 Lady Caroline Dawson wrote:

Everything seems to go in great state here, the Duchess appears in a sack and hoop and diamonds; French horns playing at every meal; and such quantities of plate et cetera one would imagine oneself in a palace. And there are servants without end . . . It is not the fashion at Carton to play cards, the ladies sit and work, and the gentlemen lollop about and go to sleep – at least the Duke does, for he snored so loud one night that we all got into a great fit of laughing and waked him.

The following year, another visitor, Miss Sandford, noted that 'the house is crowded, a thousand comes and goes' and that 'we breakfast between ten and eleven, though it is called half-past nine'. However, the second Duke also found time to support Catholic Emancipation in the House of Lords and to protest on behalf of the United Irishmen, on which count he was so popular that he was considered – had the circumstances arisen – as a possible king of Ireland. Despite the acclaim accorded to the second Duke it was his younger brother, Lord Edward FitzGerald, whose heroism gave him the reputation of Ireland's greatest patriot. After being dismissed from the army in 1792 for proposing a toast 'for the speedy abolition of hereditary titles and feudal distinctions' – he was partly inspired in this by a period spent with an Indian tribe in America – he joined the United Irishmen and organized the purchase of arms and ammunition with the intention of leading a massive uprising in May 1798. Government spies discovered the plan, and a £1,000 reward was announced for Lord Edward's capture; Castlereagh advised the second Duke to send his brother back to America without delay. But Lord Edward was determined to remain in Ireland and before long he was apprehended. He shot one assailant and stabbed another, but in the struggle he was wounded in the arm. The wound festered and he died in prison in Dublin on 4 June crying, 'Dear Ireland! I die for you!' After his death Lord Edward, though never convicted, was branded for high treason by a Bill of Attainder and to this day he is revered as a martyr to the cause.

In the nineteenth century the Dukes of Leinster set an example to Irish landowners in their fairness to their tenants, especially during the Famine. They could never be described as absentee landlords. After the Land Purchase Act of 1885 the fourth Duke offered to sell his tenants their holdings, but his offer was rejected: the FitzGeralds had shown the Irish how to stand up for themselves and the Irish responded by standing up against the FitzGeralds. In 1887 Gerald FitzGerald succeeded as fifth Duke of Leinster. He was small, like most of the family, and homely in character; any glamour in his life derived from his wife, Lady Hermione Duncombe, widely regarded as the most beautiful woman of her day. The Duke died at the age of forty-two in December 1893, Hermione little more than a year afterwards, aged only thirty. According to *Burke's Peerage* the fifth Duke and Duchess left three sons: Maurice, who succeeded to the title as sixth Duke and whose death, unmarried, was reported in 1922; Desmond, who died, also unmarried, in France in 1916; and Edward, afterwards seventh Duke of Leinster.

Lord Edward FitzGerald was born in London in May 1892. It was widely believed he was the son of Hugo Charteris, Lord Elcho, later the eleventh Earl of Wemyss. Whatever the case, he was, like many ducal indiscretions, accepted and brought up as one of the family. Houses were large, staff plentiful, and such children, provided an heir or two already existed, were easily integrated. Infant mortality might put such a son in line to succeed, but it was not through infant mortality that Lord Edward came into the dukedom.

He had no restraining parental influence as a child and, with the law of primogeniture effectively releasing him from the restrictions and responsibilities of the head of a ducal family, threw himself into a carefree youth. He was handsome, adventurous, titled; life was going to be fun. From his earliest days Edward established a reputation for wild behaviour, and he never lost it. Almost all of his eighty-three years were spent in an electric storm of publicity; he was an object of amusement to the world, embarrassment to his fellow peers, ridicule in the courts of law, derision in the House of Commons and outrage in his own family.

But on his death he was remembered for one particular act which was so spectacularly rash that the countless follies which made up his long life paled beside it. While in his twenties, heir presumptive to the Leinster fortune, he had gambled his inheritance away, only to pass the rest of his days in near poverty, hiding from the press and his creditors. Instead of enjoying an estimated income of £1,000 a week he subsisted, from the day in February 1922 when he succeeded his brother, on £1,000 a year. Although Edward later denied that he was much of a gambler, this was patently absurd. Two of his wives described his room ankle-deep in form books, bookies' slips and football pool coupons; it was clear that he would bet on anything that moved.

Before the end of the First World War Edward was in debt to the tune of £15,000 which, since he had fallen foul of money-lenders, involved repayment of about £60,000. He was in bad trouble. The trustees of the Leinster estates, from whom he received an allowance, refused to intervene; Carey Street was just round the corner. It was then that Edward was introduced to a charming, rich parvenu called Sir Harry Mallaby-Deeley. A barrister by training, Sir Harry was an MP, a vigorous raiser of war loans and the founder of the Fifty Shilling Tailors. Born Harry Deeley, he had taken his mother's maiden name and added it to his own. Edward later described him as 'well-dressed, shrewd and charming'; the gossip-columnists called him 'England's picturesquest millionaire' and an 'intrepid speculator'. Edward's second wife described him as 'a professional buyer-upper of estates on the rocks'.

Sir Harry had money and desired more; Edward had no money but golden prospects. To both men a gamble was the spice of life. In January 1918 an agreement was worked out: Sir Harry would pay off Edward's debts of £67,500 and make him a tax-free allowance of £1,000 a year for life; in return, Sir Harry would become the recipient of all income from the estates entailed with the dukedom (over £50,000 a year) but only after Edward inherited from his brother Maurice, the sixth Duke. The spin of the wheel, the turn of the card on which all hung, was the expectation of life of the sixth Duke, still in his early thirties, and, to a lesser extent, that of Edward himself. Prudently, Sir Harry insured Edward's life for £300,000 and wrote into the sequence of agreements between himself, Edward's trustee in bankruptcy and Edward certain provisos governing the latter's more madcap activities. A final agreement, summing up all previous ones, came into force on 14 September 1920. It mentions an action brought by Edward against Mallaby-Deeley in 1918 'claiming among other things that the Principal and other hereinbefore recited Agreements should be rescinded and cancelled' but this attempt at disentangling himself had come to nothing; the court had ruled that the original agreements should stand. Edward was never in a position to take advantage of a clause in the final agreement which said that at any time during the ten years following the first agreement in 1918 he could buy the reversionary rights for £400,000. The trustees of the Leinster Estates were at one point prepared to offer a quarter of a million but Sir Harry, said to be in financial difficulties of his own, would not lower the figure. In any case he soon mortgaged the reversionary rights to the Legal and General Assurance Company to raise further money, and he thus no longer received the income.

Barely two years after the agreement with Mallaby-Deeley came into force, when Edward was on holiday with a girlfriend in Italy, he received word that the sixth Duke had died. He did not return for the funeral; he later said, 'There was no point.' Although he was now seventh Duke of Leinster, and the Premier Duke, Marquess and Earl in the Peerage of Ireland, Mallaby-Deeley had his life interest in Carton, one of Ireland's greatest houses, and Kilkea, Ireland's oldest inhabited castle, as well as the use of all the family possessions. Sir Harry wisely chose to stay in his comfortable mansion in Surrey rather than visit Ireland: it was said that he would have been shot if he had set foot there.

The financial relief accorded by Mallaby-Deeley was only temporary. Nothing could induce Edward to change his ways, and during the next forty years he went bankrupt three times. Mallaby-Deeley's initial payment of £67,500 was only the tip of the iceberg. The income from the Leinster Estates was protected from the claims of Edward's creditors; in order to discharge as many of his debts as possible the trustees auctioned eighty per cent of the heirlooms (these obviously brought in no income) including all the family jewellery, most of the silver and a great many paintings and pieces of furniture. In 1926 twenty-one furniture vans containing Leinster possessions were bought by William Randolph Hearst and removed from Carton to his castle at San Simeon in California.

By the time Edward became seventh Duke he already had one broken marriage behind him. At the age of twenty-one he proposed to a pretty chorus-girl May Juanita Etheridge, the 'Pink Pajama Girl' of the Shaftesbury Theatre. The

FitzGeralds were vigorously opposed to the match, and summarily dispatched him to New Zealand. But, as one of Edward's subsequent wives put it, 'the one certain way to make him do something was to tell him he must not'. He returned and married May at Wandsworth Registry Office. 'I wasn't in love with her,' he admitted casually later, and they only lived together for a couple of years. They spent the summer of 1913 honeymooning in Canada, and on their return to England Edward – having been obliged to resign from the Irish Guards the previous year – joined the West Riding Regiment. In May 1914 they had a son, Gerald, whom May would take with her to the nightclub where she worked.

Edward returned from the war after being wounded in 1915, but he did not spend much time with his wife; instead he began rebuilding his debts. The infant Gerald was soon made a ward of court by the FitzGeralds; he lived in Ireland and later went to Eton. His mother was paid a small allowance by the FitzGeralds and asked not to use the family name or see her son, except on specified occasions. She and Edward were finally divorced in 1930 and five years later, after a period of loneliness and penury, May committed suicide.

Edward proposed to his second wife in America, where he had been sent by Mallaby-Deeley to 'woo and win a millionairess'. He had almost ensnared a middle-aged lady with the appropriate requirements when he fell in love with Raffaelle Van Neck.

In her book *So Brief a Dream* Raffaelle wrote that she 'hadn't a bean and, what's more, he knew it' and that she only discovered Edward was an undischarged bankrupt when staying with his aunt Nesta after their wedding in 1932. Lady Nesta FitzGerald was then living alone at Carton, courtesy of Mallaby-Deeley, with the help of only a handful of servants. Edward's marriage to Raffaelle was not dissolved until 1946,

14

but by then he had been living for some years with a considerably older woman, Jessie Smithers, formerly the wife of Lord Churston and Theodore Wessel. Jessie, better known as Denise Orme, was a fascinating woman but even she could not control Edward when she became his third Duchess. He conducted a series of liaisons, one of which resulted in the birth of another son, Adrian FitzGerald, in 1952.

As the years reeled by Edward's life remained unchanged: the irresponsibility, the obsessive gambling, the dodging of creditors. At one of his earliest court cases, found guilty of obtaining credit on false pretences, he suffered the humiliation of a stern rebuke from the judge: 'We treat everyone alike in these courts.' But even this, and the embarrassing publicity it generated, did not prevent Edward from exploiting the virtually unlimited credit a Duke could command. In *So Brief a Dream* Raffaelle described how her then husband always managed to get hold of a Rolls or a Bentley; despite seventeen different abodes in three years they 'lived in comparative style and comfort, though not anything like other dukes'. In 1957 readers of the *Sunday Dispatch* were regaled with a series of ghost-written confessions of the seventh Duke of Leinster, *My Forty Years of Folly*, with such headlines as 'A Bookie Backed Me to Find a Wife with One Million Pounds' and 'A Gamble that is Still Costing Me a Thousand Pounds a Week'. The tacit assumption throughout the series of articles was that Edward's escapades, purposeless and infantile enough, were somehow rendered more scandalous, more amazing, and even more acceptable, on account of his title. The episode entitled 'The Car Drive that Made MPs Call Me a Madman' was the story of a successful attempt to drive from London to Aberdeen in less time than the express train, for which he won £3,000, but was summonsed for failing to produce a driving licence. Within the week he was twice fined for speeding and, when his licence was eventually tracked down, it showed convictions dating back to 1914.

The emphasis in the articles was on Edward's escapades and he spoke little of his family; but in reference to his contract with Mallaby-Deeley he is quoted as saying:

> I was free of debt at last, but I had doubts about the future. My brother was the sixth Duke and I was his heir. As a result of an accident he was in a condition similar to a man who has been severely shell-shocked, and he could not have children. I was bound to succeed . . . and inherit the family fortune, which was estimated at between £800,000 and £1 million. Gradually it became obvious that he was failing. I knew my gamble had not come off. . . .

Before Jessie died in 1960 Edward had settled down happily with Vivien Connor, who in 1964 became his fourth and last Duchess. They had met when the Duke was living, as Mr FitzGerald, in a block of flats where Vivien was the landlady. The press had always given Edward good coverage, but ten years after the *Sunday Dispatch* confessions the mood of the headlines had changed: 'Living on Baked Beans We Dodged the Creditors' announced the *News of the World* in 1967. It was only through Vivien's hard work and her insistence that they lived within their means that Edward was finally discharged from bankruptcy. On his part, Edward made some effort to earn a living; he crocheted costumes for young ice skaters and devised plans for selling plots of historic England – none of which he owned – to Americans. He was required by law to wait six years after being discharged from bankruptcy to apply for a Writ of Summons to the House of Lords. He had then to produce family birth and death certificates and a signed affidavit from his first cousin, Sir Fergus Graham, to the effect that he was his father's son.

In 1975 Edward emerged once more into the limelight. He was photographed in his rented robes attending his first Opening of Parliament, a tall, gaunt, long-haired figure holding the coronet of the Viscounts of Leinster which his son had recently found in a box bearing the words 'Last worn at the Coronation of George III'. Beside him stood his fourth wife, Vivien, in a new Dior dress and a borrowed tiara. When asked how often he would attend the House of Lords he said, 'Two or three times a week. There is some money in it, isn't there? Not much, but it will help.' And what would he speak on? 'Conservation – whales, porpoises, animals – that sort of thing.' In the event he died without making his maiden speech.

The Leinster coronet was to play a leading part in the seventh Duke's last public fiasco. He became involved in a charitable project called the All Ireland Distress Fund which aimed to bring orphans of the fighting, both Protestant and Catholic, to homes in England. Although Vivien was opposed to the whole venture, they were persuaded to embark on a publicity trip to America financed by certain unnamed trustees of the Fund. But the whole scheme came to nothing. They did not have the necessary permit to collect for charity in America, although a novel idea for a collecting-box was worked out: a slit would be made in the coronet's box through which the admiring Americans would push dollar bills. As the Duke and Duchess could do nothing useful in America, the Duke insisted on going to Montreal where, to his wife's astonishment, they visited the places he had been to on his first honeymoon in 1913. They then returned to England. The trip never raised a penny, but had cost the trustees of the charity £10,000 (or so they claimed). Moreover, Edward had managed to lose his coronet somewhere along the way. It was several months before it was traced to the treasurer of the fund who, anxious to recoup some of his losses, offered to sell it back to the family. They refused.

During the many years the seventh Duke lived in a succession of council flats and bed-sitting-rooms the Mallaby-Deeleys had flourished, although after the death of Sir Harry in 1937 many of his family had met unfortunate ends in accidents or in asylums.

The Duke's only legitimate son and heir, Gerald, Marquess of Kildare, had also flourished, mainly through his own efforts. As a child he never saw his father, but he saw his mother on numerous occasions; she spent two weeks of every summer at Johnstown Castle in County Wexford, where Gerald lived with his great-aunt Adelaide. After Eton and Sandhurst he had served as an officer in the 5th Inniskilling Dragoon Guards and was severely wounded in the Second World War. His great love was flying and at the time of his father's death he was chairman of the largest general aviation company in Europe. He married twice; by his first wife he had three daughters (the eldest of whom died young), by his second two sons.

In an interview shortly before his father's death the Marquess said that he recognized that the Mallaby-Deeleys had made a good deal and his father a bad one, and blamed no one for it. He had always been on good terms with Sir Harry and his heirs, who had guaranteed his bank overdraft so that he could purchase his first plane. In 1949, when the upkeep of Carton was proving too great a charge on Leinster income, he had given his permission for the house to be sold to the brewer Lord Brocket for £80,000, in exchange for being allowed to live at Kilkea Castle with enough cash to renovate it. When, with the permission of the Trustees, Kilkea was sold in 1960 the proceeds were used to buy Langston House in Oxfordshire. The house was furnished entirely with the remaining contents of Carton and hung with family pictures which, like everything else, could be used by the Mallaby-Deeleys. On two occasions previously the Marquess had attempted to buy back his father's reversionary rights; both times, on the point of completion, the sale had fallen through.

With Edward's death the legal relationship between the FitzGeralds and the Mallaby-Deeleys ended; the family heirlooms which had long lodged with the Marquess now became his own. These included what still remained of the family portraits and plate, furniture, manuscripts and miniatures. But one significant item was missing: the portrait of Maurice, sixth Duke of Leinster, on whose reported death in 1922 the 'Bed-Sit Duke' had inherited.

The limelight had been focused for so long on the exploits of the seventh Duke that there had been no room for the shadow of his predecessor. But with the seventh Duke's death, Leonard FitzGerald was able to make his claim to the dukedom, and the shadow of the sixth Duke returned. The missing portrait was just the start of the mystery surrounding its subject. If the seventh Duke found peace in death, he was probably the only member of the family to do so.

2

Stranger than Fiction

WHEN Maurice Francis FitzGerald, the self-styled ex-Duke of Leinster, died in 1967 he left three children, of whom Leonard, born in 1929, was his heir. An art teacher by profession, Leonard was also an accomplished draughtsman, sculptor, footballer and fisherman. Before his father's death Leonard had shown little enthusiasm in substantiating the details of his life. It wasn't that he was uninterested, but he was certainly disinterested; he was a shy man and unconcerned with personal publicity or the possibility of any financial gain.

After his father's death in 1967 a number of newspapers and magazines, including *Life*, had approached him for Maurice Francis' story. On the advice of his family Leonard had withheld his co-operation, for the last thing they wanted was their father's memory disturbed by sensationalism. Nevertheless, Leonard's eldest sister, Patricia Roberts, who had always shown a greater interest in their late father's life, was not averse to some suitable testimonial being published, if the right person could be found. After all, their father had frequently repeated that he wanted to write his life story – the story of how, under pressure from his scheming, avaricious uncles and feckless younger brother Lord Edward, he had signed away all his rights to the dukedom only to pass the rest of his days far from the land of his birth as cattleman, rancher, circus performer, film extra, occasional author and, at the end, dapper retiree.

One of Patricia's friends referred her to the author Charles Graves, but with due modesty Graves demurred. Although well versed in the activities of the rich and titled, Graves said that he would not write anything himself but would pass on the relevant details to another author, Dermot Morrah, a biographer of royalty and noted genealogist, who occupied a senior post at the College of Heralds in London.

The short biography of her father Patricia sent Morrah in 1968 stated that Maurice Francis had arrived in Canada at the beginning of the century as a boy runaway from England. He had served in the Canadian Forces in the First World War, after which he had returned to Canada where, on 12 April 1919, he married Eleanor Gough by whom he had issue. At the time, it was said, he was in frequent correspondence with his brother, Lord Edward, who recognized him both as brother and authentic Duke. The brothers had last met in Montreal in January 1922 when, with the co-operation of attorneys, Maurice Francis had entered into an agreement by which he purported to abdicate the title in favour of his brother. A false statement of his death had then been fabricated and subsequently made public in England. He had changed his name, and from that time all communication had been broken off.

If this story were true, Morrah said, only three pieces of evidence were required to establish Leonard's claim. A certificate of the marriage to Eleanor Gough, Leonard's birth certificate and evidence that identified the bridegroom as the person recognized by Lord Edward as his elder brother.

Although Patricia said all communication had been broken off she well remembered her father receiving letters from his family, but these had all been destroyed. At his death no correspondence between Maurice Francis and the seventh Duke was to be found among his papers, except for an incomplete letter written by the former in 1930 which had never been sent.

At the same time Patricia's stepsister (a daughter by a previous marriage of Maurice Francis' third wife, then in hospital) engaged a firm of solicitors in London who suggested a further line of enquiry. The important detail, they felt, was to establish the identity of the man who had died in 1922 and the circumstances of his death and burial. Morrah had not raised this point; from the story he had been told by Patricia he must have assumed that no one had died in that year. The solicitors pointed out to Patricia's stepsister that the Leinster family had once owned sixty thousand acres in Ireland but were now bankrupt, and that the matter should be referred to a specialist who handled many peerage claims. The peerage specialist told her that were a claim made it would be referred to the Lord Chancellor who, if he was not satisfied with the seventh Duke's bona fides, would in turn refer the case to a House of Lords committee. In the case of a non-British or non-Irish subject the Writ of Summons would not be issued. If Leonard were acknowledged rightful Duke he would be sent a letter to that effect but would not be able to sit in the House of Lords. Although five of the Leinster titles are in the Peerage of Ireland, holders of which do not sit of right in the House of Lords, the Dukes of Leinster sit in the House of Lords under their English viscountcy. The specialist reiterated that the evidence the Americans had so far produced did not establish such a claim, but added that the House of Lords had received a letter during the 1930s declaring Leonard to be the rightful heir, but the matter had not been pursued at the time – who had written the letter was not made known. He had also located the will of the sixth Duke, whose personal estate had amounted to £24,000. Nothing had come to light regarding a pension for widows of the Dukes of Leinster of which Maurice Francis had spoken and which was the reason for the stepsister's involvement. Patricia was reluctant to spare any more money on behalf of her stepmother, and her stepsister was also unwilling to shoulder further costs; soon afterwards, the peerage specialist and Maurice's widow both died.

Leonard himself remained dubious, and admitted that he had long been sceptical of his father's tales. This was largely due to the unfortunate circumstances of his childhood – at the time of his parents' separation in 1930 he was only a year old – and the antipathy of his stepfather to Maurice Francis. But it was also thanks to his father's heavy-handedness. Leonard was sixteen before he spent so much as three weeks with Maurice Francis; when, on his return from army service as a paratrooper with the American Occupation Forces in Japan, Leonard said he wanted to go to college his father curtly dismissed the idea – he was not, he said, bright enough – and suggested he find a job. It was hardly the kind of encouragement an inadequately educated but gifted young man could be expected to welcome. Not surprisingly he rebuffed his father when soon after he was asked if he was interested in assuming the courtesy title 'Marquess of Kildare'.

Yet now his father was dead Leonard wondered if it was only because he had been young and impetuous that he had refused to listen to his father. After all, everyone – except his stepfather – had seen him as an honourable man, a true gentleman. People remarked especially on his wonderful manners, his dignity, his old-world habits. Only the best was good enough for him. Perhaps his father's father had indeed been a duke, the premier nobleman of all Ireland? Yet he had thrown it all over and run away. Who might not have under such pressure as his father described? And not merely to run away, but to create a new life in a strange country – one could admire any man for that. There was so much Leonard now wanted and needed to know – he felt not only guilty but ungrateful. His father had wanted to tell him so many things but he just had not wanted to listen then.

Leonard did remember how before her death his mother frequently said that it was largely on account of Maurice Francis' family that she had divorced him. They were driving her crazy, having her followed, even trying to kidnap her children. His sister Theresa remembered how as a child she had been taken away by her parents and hidden; Leonard himself recalled sudden long train journeys when night and day merged in his infant mind. Leonard had also heard how in 1913 his father was receiving a yearly allowance from England, but it had evidently stopped before his birth. According to Patricia, their mother said it amounted to as much as ten thousand dollars in the first years of their marriage. But Leonard himself had no recollection of the expensive treats and holidays, the summer and winter homes, the picnics, the servants, the new automobiles which Patricia could recall so vividly. He could only remember the orphanage in Tucson, Arizona, into which he and his other sister, Theresa, had been put while their parents wrangled bitterly over the divorce. A great many years later, when Maurice Francis had gone to live with his son, it had not been easy for either of them. In time, though, their relationship had improved; Leonard had become less hot-headed. It wasn't that he didn't want to believe his father, he simply didn't know how to. A self-confessed 'redneck' who believed in the American way of life he was only interested in his father for what he had done, not from whence he came.

In 1963, shortly before Leonard left for a holiday, Maurice Francis made one further concerted attempt to interest his son in his heritage. Leonard had not responded. 'Well,' his father said, 'if you ever decide to, it's all there.' And when Leonard had a son, Paul Maurice, it was on him that Maurice Francis focused all his hopes for the future, and to Patricia that he turned for reassurance that his wishes would be met.

When Maurice Francis married for the third time in 1964, he moved away from Leonard's house. Three years later, while sitting up in a hospital bed, he suffered a lung haemorrhage and died. Maurice Francis had been in hospital for some time, visited daily by Patricia, who had seen him on the morning of his death. Leonard had not been there at the end, and for that he felt added guilt.

Leonard's eldest sister, Mrs Patricia Roberts, never shared his doubts. At the time of their father's death Patricia was in her late forties, the mother of two young children. After suffering two heart attacks in her late twenties she had forsaken a nursing career for a less arduous domestic life. Very happily married to a retired Air Force colonel, Glen Roberts, she remained an active, talkative woman – effusive, contented, self-sufficient – with a deep affection for her father and a great interest in the details of his former life. While Leonard's feelings towards his father were ambivalent and his attitude to the stories sceptical, Patricia, on the other hand, had an unwavering devotion to her father and his memory and was quite unable to consider the possibility that he had invented past experiences. During the years following his death it was her tenacity and determination that maintained the momentum in the search for truth, but her love and adoration for her father laid her open to inconsistency and self-deception.

Shortly before his death Maurice Francis had told Patricia, 'When I die, notify my brother Ted who lives in Sussex, and he will discreetly take care of everything from there.' He also told her, and Leonard, that when he died it was imperative that his fingerprints were taken and registered.

So Patricia had cabled the news to the seventh Duke, but her telegram had been returned as 'not delivered'. That it had been opened, however, was quite clear to her, for the telegram had been sent from 'Mrs G. S. Roberts' and returned to 'Patricia Roberts'. With the return of the telegram Patricia's life took on a new dimension: she became little less than a woman with a mission and immediately had her father's fingerprints registered.

Maurice Francis had been a private man. He had rarely spoken outside his immediate family of his life before leaving England, but in his last years Patricia had attempted to make a record for posterity. Whenever possible she had questioned him, recording the results on tape. Now she resolved to fill the gaps in her father's stories as best she could, and she canvassed family and friends for any recollections they might have.

Of all the conversations with her father one in particular stood out in her mind, for it had been on a special occasion, his eightieth birthday, and, though no one knew it at the time, it was to be his last. The first of March – for years the date had been a family joke. For just as during his early years in America he had frequently changed his name, so too had he provided a variety of birth dates to match his different identities. When as 'Francis FitzGerald' he had joined the Canadian Overseas Expeditionary Force in June 1916 he had specified 24 January 1887. But, in at least one passport under the name of Maurice Francis FitzGerald, Patricia remembered seeing her father's date of birth as 10 June 1888. When quizzed about these discrepancies and why he now used 1 March, he said, 'Well, it's my actual birthday and it's between the two anyway.' Now, when such information was vital, it did not seem as funny. Nothing did.

Nevertheless, 1 March 1967 had been the date of the celebration. After it was over Maurice Francis had stayed for a few days with Patricia, talking to her for hours about his family, his childhood, his youthful dreams, his regrets. She didn't tell her father she was recording him, and tried to hide the whirring of the tape-recorder (which was hidden under a sofa) with the noise from the television.

Of all the things he mentioned, one remark stood out from the rest, for it seemed to her to sum up her father so well – his modesty, integrity, honour: he asked his family to remember that as a young man he had made a solemn promise never to reveal a terrible family secret, and he had never broken it. He had then added that 'soon the title would no longer rightfully be mine' – something which Patricia would never forget.

As he had done on previous occasions, Patricia's father talked about his parents, Hermione Wilhelmina Duncombe, daughter of the first Earl of Feversham, and Gerald FitzGerald, fifth Duke of Leinster, where they were from, where they were married, where and from what causes they died. But there was a new piece of information this time, one which was to play a vital part in the research of the next few years. Of this marriage, Maurice Francis said, there had been four children, all boys. Patricia remonstrated that according to the reference books she had seen there had been only Maurice, Desmond and Edward. But he said, 'Damn it, dear, have it your own way if you wish. There were still four boys – I should know, I was there. Just don't believe everything you read, just listen, and listen well, please. . . .'

· · · · ·

Maurice Francis, it appeared, was not the eldest but the second child. The eldest had apparently been a sickly child named Frederick. An invalid from birth, he had been kept in a locked room on the third floor at Carton, his existence unknown to all but a few. After Maurice came Desmond, who died in France in 1916, then Edward, who had become the seventh Duke.

Hermione, beautiful, talented, affectionate, doomed – the most romantic of mothers – had died when Maurice Francis was only eight years old, but she had gone out of his life before then. It happened very suddenly in March 1895 from complications of typhoid and tuberculosis. Maurice Francis added that he guessed 'she died from a broken heart as well'. She was quite tall, with auburn hair and dark grey-blue eyes, in which features Maurice Francis claimed to resemble her – although he had lost his hair and his eyes had become much paler after suffering mustard gas poisoning in the trenches. Both the Duncombe and FitzGerald families had been opposed to the marriage, and had tried to have it annulled after his birth, but the attempt had failed because his parents were very much in love. The FitzGeralds, he thought, were jealous of Hermione, who was as beautiful as they were plain. At the time of her death she had been a widow for fifteen months, the fifth Duke having died in December 1893 of typhoid fever contracted from contaminated oysters cooked in a copper kettle. He had been ill off and on for two years. Maurice could not recall much about his father, except that he had been kind and had taught him to swim and play the violin.

Maurice Francis said he was born on 1 March 1887 at Kilkea Castle. The ancient building, a tiny fairy castle with four tall turrets, had been given by the fifth Duke to his spinster sisters and brother Walter to live in during their lifetime. It had previously been a hunting lodge, Maurice Francis said.

The FitzGeralds were a large family. One uncle, George, was in the diplomatic service and usually lived in Italy; another, Frederick, was a stern ex-army officer who ran the family affairs and was head of the clan after the fifth Duke's death in 1893; a confirmed bachelor, he lived at Carton. Aunt Alice, the eldest daughter, was rather bossy, but sympathetic towards Maurice Francis. Her husband was also a military man and they had two daughters. There was another uncle, Lord Henry, living in Somerset, whom Maurice Francis disliked. When he was deported from America in 1930 Maurice Francis told Patricia he had only to write to this uncle, who had something to do with public records, to receive new papers.

When they visited Kilkea, Maurice Francis remembered, he and his brothers would be dressed up in little suits with velvet collars. On reaching the gates they would jump out of the carriage and forage around the grounds. Their friends the Kavanaghs lived on one side, the Jacksons close by; there were also the Traverses and the Inglises, people working on the estate, who had children with whom they might play. When they reached the castle they would often be dirty and, rather than using the front door, they would enter by the dairy where Brigid or some other maid would make them presentable. Much of the forest at Kilkea, in which they built tree-houses and forts, was virgin timber uncut for centuries. Although his cousins were sometimes there, usually only he and Desmond would play. The others would stay up at the castle with their nurse, Marianne Timmins. Maurice Francis and his brother would sometimes poach on their own land; the gamekeeper, Mr Inglis, occasionally caught them.

The older boy, Frederick, had required constant care. Maurice Francis was at times not even sure whether he was a brother, a cousin or the illegitimate son of one of the uncles, but he assumed he was a brother because he knew himself to be the second child. 'There were so many stories,' he said. He thought that the reason for secrecy was shame. Rarely allowed to play with Frederick, Maurice Francis said he vividly recalled the boy's screams when, on one occasion he bumped against a bedpost. 'I had nightmares about it,' he said, 'and as per usual I got the blame.' When he was punished for it by being hit across the face with a riding crop, aunt Alice took his part, and this caused a major family row. Through some incapacity Frederick had to be carried everywhere and suffered constant pain. He was said to have 'soft bones' as well as what sounded to Patricia like the childish form of epilepsy, *petit mal*. Later he became increasingly hard to handle and had to have strong attendants. Eventually he was placed in a sanatorium in the north of Ireland.

With Desmond, on the other hand, Maurice Francis was as thick as thieves. 'We were always in mischief,' he said. 'I usually got the blame, however. You see, they suspected me right away, whereas Desmond could do no wrong – he was the gentleman of the family. It didn't matter where he was concerned. We were the best of friends . . . Ted? Oh, he wasn't very bright. He was much younger and wasn't around very much. He was more the age of our cousins. As he grew up he was selfish and demanding. I always said he'd make a mess of things, and he certainly did.' Their mother had once said she was bringing up 'three gentlemen and one banshee' and had added, 'Whatever is going to happen to you?' Maurice Francis also thought that because he looked like his mother the FitzGerald side of the family took such a dislike to him.

On their mother's death the children were put under the guardianship of their father's brother, Lord Frederick Fitz-Gerald, and their mother's sister, Lady Cynthia Graham. Maurice Francis remembered giving her a prayer-book. The many Fitzgerald aunts and uncles 'were always arguing on any subject from politics to our being disciplined. It was like a madhouse. I would often go to the library or my room to read.' Although he had not spent much time at Carton he remembered the magnificent library and the privately printed history of the FitzGeralds written by his grandfather, the fourth Duke, and an original copy of *The Rubaiyat of Omar Khayyam* translated by a cousin, which were always displayed on a table.

Maurice Francis said he had been 'designated Marquess of Kildare' on his father's death in 1893 but, although educated to succeed to the title, he knew it belonged to someone else. He had been baptised in the Anglican church at Maynooth, but couldn't remember the names of his godparents. He thought he attended the same school as his uncle Walter. He remembered being visited there by his aunts Alice FitzGerald and Helen Vincent; the school had been some way south of London. Then he went to a public school between Fareham and Gosport in Hampshire. It was close to the Isle of Wight and he had stayed with his uncle, who lived there. Later he went to Eton. He recalled a master called Beard whose son, Johnny, was in his class.

As a result of Frederick's 'incapacity' the duties of the Duke had, according to Maurice Francis, devolved upon him. He had acted as train-bearer at the Coronation of Edward VII in 1902. There had been endless hours of practice. At one point in the ceremony he had had to kneel before the King and Queen and raise his coronet above his head. He remembered Queen Alexandra, tall, slim and regal, smiling at him. At this point he was a schoolboy at Eton. His health was not good; he suffered from asthma and it was feared that, like his mother, he might be consumptive; travel was recommended. In fact, he had always been encouraged to travel. When quite young he and a brother had stayed with relatives in India, and he remembered being ill when staying in Rawalpindi with a Colonel Menzies, a close friend of his parents. Several close relations had served out there and one of his uncles had been Governor of Bombay. His uncles and father, Maurice Francis said, had once belonged to the King's Royal Rifle Corps. As a child he had been interested in history and geography and was therefore happy to visit all the places of which he had read. He did not travel under any title, he told Patricia, but under the name of Maurice FitzGerald. When quite young he had visited Malta and Mauritius, and had toured Australia in 1907 and Egypt in 1909. Usually he had been accompanied by friends, relations or a personal physician, among whom was Captain Rose – a retired sea captain who was connected with Brompton Hospital, where Maurice Francis had been treated for his chest – and, later, Dr Pollock. There was also a companion called Captain Rayleigh, a friend of his father's, whom he had liked best. Maurice Francis also remembered going with Desmond on 'a grand tour of Scotland Yard, where a relative of my aunt Helen Duncombe was in charge of an office. I think his name was Vincent.' They both had their fingerprints taken. Maurice Francis also said his fingerprints had been taken on other occasions, once in connection with a trip to India and once in France.

When he was twenty, Maurice Francis said, he was sent on a world tour, and returned to Kilkea for his coming of age celebrations – although he knew he could not inherit while his elder brother survived. In the meantime his uncles were 'busy feathering their own nests' and 'splitting it all among themselves'. In 1903 and 1905 many Leinster properties had been sold but the proceeds, rather than being invested, were apportioned among the FitzGeralds. This had been arranged by a distant relation named Wyndham, an MP. Maurice Francis felt he should have some say in matters when he came of age but he was powerless against the uncles. 'Because of my position,' he told Patricia, 'I always had to do as they wished. I was resentful as a teenager; I even ran away from school a few times. I had no life of my own. They wanted me to be their puppet.' In July 1908 he was made to sign over some of the properties to relations, including 10 Carlton House Terrace, London, to his brother Ted, and make a will. He wasn't allowed to apply for a Writ of Summons because of his health, yet his uncles wanted him to join the navy. They even enrolled him in a naval school in Scotland, but Maurice Francis preferred the army and when he ran away to Canada he joined the Missigia Light Horse. Maurice Francis had the impression that his uncles wanted to cut him out of the succession so that the title could go to Desmond, but Desmond had not wanted it unless it came to him rightfully. Maurice Francis said his guardians had told him he was 'a zealous if sick young man' and in 1910 or 1911 his uncle Frederick had him examined after a fainting spell by a 'mental practitioner'. In 1913 he had treatment 'for his chest' in Edinburgh.

Maurice Francis' boyhood reading had consisted largely of adventure tales of the Wild West and he had seen Buffalo Bill Cody's travelling circus on its 1903 British tour. He had been taught to ride by aunt Helen's husband, Edgar Vincent, and he heard about several cousins – the Sutherlands and Douglases – who had settled in Colorado, Montana, Wyoming and Texas. Unhappy and frustrated, he finally decided to run away to Canada. The actual year he left was uncertain; Maurice Francis was nothing if not vague in his old age. 'Everything was arranged for me, and I left by night,' he said, his aunts Cynthia, Ada and Alice providing the necessary funds. He said he continued to receive an allowance from aunt Cynthia until her death in 1926. But running away held terrors he had not

34

anticipated: 'I was frightened, as I was on my own then. I later assumed the name Charlie Tyler. I had gone to school with some Tyler boys from South Wales. I survived and learned to love my new life . . . I eventually went to work on a large cattle ranch where they recruited English boys; I worked hard, but it certainly agreed with me.'

Later he joined Buffalo Bill's circus, with which he toured as a stunt rider, only to discover his hero was a fraud. Then in St Louis, Missouri, he left the circus and took a job training polo ponies at the local country club.

At this point Maurice Francis' story became even more confused. On various occasions Patricia remembered her father saying that he had attended cavalry school in Toronto, that he had worked for a bank and on the Montreal Stock Exchange. Perhaps he had done all three. It seemed impossible to compile an exact chronology of these years, but Patricia could testify to her father's skill at playing the stock market and his splendid horsemanship. Whatever the exact details, he at one point lived in Meeteetsee, a small town in Wyoming, before organizing a quiet honeymoon for Edward and May in Montreal in May or June 1913; he then worked for Buffalo Bill's circus. When the circus closed he trained polo ponies at the St Louis Country Club, and in mid 1914 he organized a trip by packhorse through Yellowstone Park for some friends; in 1915 they made a similar trip during which he was severely injured falling from a horse. He was sent to Denver for treatment, after which, he said, he returned to England. In March 1916, while he was there, news of Lord Desmond's death reached him. At the news he decided to drop the name Charlie Tyler and call himself Maurice FitzGerald again.

He crossed the Atlantic once more, and, as America had not yet joined the war, he went to Canada to join up. While awaiting a commission he heard of the death of a cousin,

Colonel Arthur Oswald FitzGerald, Kitchener's ADC. 'Another good FitzGerald gone,' thought Maurice Francis, and signed up on that very day, 5 June 1916, in the Fort Garry Horse. When asked by Patricia why he had joined the army under the name 'Francis FitzGerald' he gave the slightly anomalous reply that he 'was damned if he was going to die under an assumed name'.

On 6 July he sailed for England and while there made a couple of visits to his family, who showed much surprise at his Canadian uniform. He saw his favourite uncle, Hubert Duncombe, and Lord Edward's wife May with her little son Gerald. Lord Edward had not been there and Maurice Francis told Patricia he was shocked to find May almost destitute, receiving no money from the family and being harassed by the uncles to give up her son. In February 1917 he embarked for France, took part in the last cavalry charge – at Cambrai – and was twice awarded the Military Medal for valour. He was discharged from the army in Canada in November 1918, and went to America for treatment for mustard gas poisoning. Soon after this he met Eleanor Gough, the daughter of a wealthy English mine-owner. Giving up the idea of going to art school in Chicago she followed Maurice Francis back to Canada where, on 12 April 1919, they were married. She was only fifteen at the time. Maurice Francis said he was uncertain as to what he should do next, so he tossed a coin. He decided to homestead on land offered to him as a war veteran, and he subsequently bought another farm.

Shortly after his marriage, Maurice Francis said, two momentous events occurred: the death of the invalid Frederick and his own 'abdication' from the Leinster titles. Apparently Edward had long been clamouring to succeed – 'he kept on asking me and begging me; I said no many times' – and Maurice Francis finally capitulated. The brothers met in

Montreal where they came to a curious agreement whereby
Maurice Francis would take the place of the recently deceased
Frederick, handing over the ducal rights to Edward for a
consideration, while Edward, on his part, agreed never to
apply for a Writ of Summons. In spite of this Edward would in
the eyes of the world be both *de jure* and *de facto* the seventh
Duke of Leinster. As far as the FitzGeralds were concerned,
Maurice Francis was now legally dead. Concerning this extraordinary part of his life Patricia's father was at his most vague;
he intimated to Patricia that, whatever else he had done, he
had kept the 'terrible family secret' to himself all his life, and
she assumed that the details of the arrangement with Edward
were part of it.

Maurice Francis said he had proved the family wrong over
one thing. He had been told he was unable to have children and
although three of his children did die in infancy three survived,
the last of whom was Leonard. Maurice Francis was confident
that if his children were to follow up his story, the truth would
out. He often told them that ample evidence existed to establish
his 'true identity'.

With these reminiscences, and recollections gathered from his
surviving friends, Patricia attempted to piece together a precise
record of her father's life.

There was one clue she could follow: Maurice Francis had
told them that, if they wanted to know the truth, they should go
to the Tyler family. But, like the returned telegram, this was to
prove a dead end. Patricia checked with the Eton College
Register and found a George Edward Tyler from Glamorgan,
South Wales, who had been at the school with the sixth Duke of
Leinster. When she contacted his family it transpired that he
had died before the Second World War and his surviving
relations knew nothing of Maurice Francis FitzGerald.

In 1971 Patricia came to London to further her researches. Anxious to meet the seventh Duke, but unsure of his whereabouts at the time, she telephoned his first cousin, Brigadier Denis FitzGerald, youngest son of Lord Henry, the fifth Duke's youngest brother. A meeting was arranged, but the day after she spoke to him she received a telephone call from him informing her that no possible familial relationship could exist between them and that the arranged meeting was therefore superfluous. However, she was able to make contact with a nephew of the fifth Duchess, a son of Hubert Duncombe, her father's favourite uncle, who confirmed distinct physical resemblances between Maurice Francis and members of the Duncombe family.

While she was in Britain Patricia took the opportunity of going to Ireland. Although unable to see Carton she visited Kilkea, by then a hotel. She told her family that she located a number of the 'tree forts' which her father had remembered playing in as a boy and, within the castle itself, a secret door of which the present owners were ignorant.

But Patricia was only too aware of the gaps in the story. Everything she knew was circumstantial; she had no proof. For the last few years of his life her father had lived apart from his children and, as was his habit, ever meticulous, he had destroyed many papers. There were a couple of trunks filled with an odd assortment of treasures ranging from used envelopes and old postcards to pieces of jewellery, coins and medals. Patricia found a bundle of newspaper clippings concerning the seventh Duke of Leinster dating back to 1922, and original sepiatones of Hermione, Duchess of Leinster, and of Lord Desmond FitzGerald, but it was obviously going to be quite a job sorting out all these effects. She would deal with them when she had more time.

When Eleanor Gough, Patricia's mother, had died in 1953,

her belongings had been scattered or destroyed. Some years earlier, Maurice's second wife had taken a number of his possessions and, with misplaced largesse, had distributed them indiscriminately. Maurice Francis himself said that in 1916, when he returned to Meeteetse from England, he had found his cabin broken into and many of his most prized possessions stolen. In view of his frequent changes of address it was difficult, particularly after his death, to know where any of his belongings might be. Patricia thought he might perhaps have placed essential evidence in a safe deposit box or with a lawyer; it would have been absolutely in character for him to do so either out of mischievousness or, less selfishly, to conceal some terrible secret. Although she remembered how he had always kept copies of all letters he wrote, however trivial, he had been equally thorough in destroying all correspondence with his family. Patricia also felt that her father, aware of Leonard's apparent disbelief and intractability, had not wanted to make it easy for his son if he ever wanted to press a claim of any sort.

Patricia had implicit faith in her father, but it was not until 1975, when he heard that the seventh Duke had taken his seat in the House of Lords, that Leonard changed his attitude. This move flagrantly disregarded the terms of the 'abdication agreement' of which his father had spoken, in that Edward had agreed never to apply for a Writ of Summons. Shocked and outraged, Leonard decided to make his claim known to the authorities concerned. But when the Lord Chancellor's Office wrote back to him they said the matter was closed, because the issuing of the Writ of Summons itself created a peerage which could only be revoked by an act of parliament. This was the first official notification Leonard received that his claim to the dukedom would not be easy to establish. He was thus forced to wait until the seventh Duke died before he could challenge the heir apparent, Gerald, Marquess of Kildare.

Leonard, then in his late forties, had recently suffered two massive heart attacks. His doctors had ordered him to rest but the thought of preparing his claim made it difficult to remain calm. His greatest fear was that he might have a fatal heart attack before the whole question was resolved and, like many people, he wished to pass on to his children something of his family's history.

Therefore, despite the initial rebuff, he instructed his solicitors to investigate the problem immediatly. It should not be too difficult, he told them, as his father had always stressed that in the event of his death it was imperative that his fingerprints be taken and registered so that his real identity could be established. Unfortunately, the solicitors were unable to trace any fingerprints belonging to the sixth Duke of Leinster with which to compare them. And before they could follow up any further lines of investigation Leonard heard that the seventh Duke had died and been succeeded by Gerald, Marquess of Kildare.

3

The Claim from California

I T was late in 1975 when Tom McGuire, a San Franciscan
schoolteacher, read a review of Brian Masters' book *The
Dukes* which mentioned the declining fortunes of the house
of Leinster since the sixth Duke's death of a brain tumour in
Edinburgh in 1922. McGuire was something of an antiquarian
and had long been interested in the British peerage; he well
remembered the obituary of the 'ex-Duke of Leinster' he had
read eight years before, in which there had been no mention of
a brain tumour. He had meant to look into it at the time but
had never got round to it. What disturbed him was this:
although American newspapers can be relied upon to get the
most insignificant fact about protocol or titles wrong, the *San
Francisco Chronicle* had been unequivocal about the 'abdication'.
McGuire knew that heirs to British titles cannot abdicate in the
way that a monarch may; if Maurice Francis FitzGerald had
indeed abdicated the dukedom of Leinster, it could only have
been done by faking his own death as his obituary had
suggested.

McGuire knew nothing of the Leinster dukedom. He could
find nothing in *Burke's Peerage* to illuminate the obituary other
than the bald statement that Maurice, sixth Duke of Leinster,
had died unmarried in 1922. He wondered, if the man who had

died in November 1967 had indeed been the sixth Duke of Leinster, how had the death been faked and why had such an 'abdication' been arranged? What could have prompted him to relinquish the premier Irish title and all that went with it? And what of the man's son, Leonard FitzGerald, mentioned in the *San Francisco Chronicle*: would he now follow up his claim for the title? It was clear from *Burke's* that the FitzGerald family had occupied a pre-eminent place in Irish history for centuries; there must be much at stake.

McGuire was always fascinated by the more colourful aspects of illustrious families. He knew, for example, that the English law of primogeniture offers ample opportunity to the imposter. The insistence on a male heir to carry on a title and the frequent entailing of estates with a title means that whole branches of a family who have enjoyed great wealth and privilege may be cut off by a single death, even ejected from their homes, if the title passes to a distant kinsman. If the obituary was correct, the seventh Duke and his son stood to lose their right to the title and any property that went with it, a story the newspapers would relish. McGuire was intrigued. He checked the acknowledgements in Masters' book and found that his information had been supplied by the seventh Duke's heir. He obtained a copy of Maurice Francis FitzGerald's death certificate, and located Leonard FitzGerald. Leonard referred him to Patricia, the family historian, and, once she was convinced of the purely disinterested nature of his concern, they met in early 1976.

Patricia passed on to McGuire the story of her father's life as she had by then pieced it together. She told him of the countless hours she had spent collating details and transcribing tapes. It was a confusing tale, uncertain in places, contradictory in others, but it was far more comprehensive than the one she had given Charles Graves or Dermot Morrah some years before.

McGuire, well aware of the problems Patricia faced, set about establishing some of the points in Maurice Francis' story. This involved checking the names of relatives, family retainers, dates and places of foreign trips, his education at Eton and his role as train-bearer at Edward VII's coronation in 1902. Using old copies of *The Times* and the *Illustrated London News* McGuire ascertained the accuracy of several of them – though this of course only demonstrated how easy it might be for an imposter to acquire information.

McGuire could not find a single reference to the sixth Duke in *The Times* after 1910. Leonard FitzGerald's solicitors had been unable to locate any medical records under the name of the Duke of Leinster at Craighouse, the place of his supposed death, after mid 1913 – the first year that Maurice Francis' whereabouts in America could with certainty be established. The entry in the Edinburgh register of deaths also supported the existence of an elder brother. It gave the sixth Duke's age at his supposed death as thirty-five, when he should have been thirty-four. It gave the causes of death as 'pneumonia ($4\frac{1}{2}$ days) and epilepsy (25 years)'. If the last figure was correct, there seemed reason to doubt that the man who died in 1922 had attended the King at his coronation, given the unpredictable nature of the complaint and the particular horror with which it was then regarded. For McGuire, the fact which was most favourable to Leonard's claim concerned the will of the sixth Duke. Maurice Francis had given his family exact details of the document which, when they finally obtained a copy years after his death, proved correct in almost every respect. He was not aware of the system in England by which anyone can buy a copy of any will lodged at Somerset House. Yet, if he were the man he claimed to be, why had he neither left palpable proof of his story nor done anything to further the rights of his own son and grandson? Though he and Leonard were never on very cordial terms, Maurice Francis had evidently shown particular concern for the dukedom after the birth of Leonard's first son.

Maurice Francis' failure to pursue his claim himself could be explained, McGuire thought, by the promise he said he had made never to reveal 'a terrible family secret'. Although Maurice Francis had not hinted at what this was, McGuire felt that it must have something to do with the mysterious elder brother. No one would have made the effort to concoct such an extraordinary story unless he believed that it could not be disproved. This may have been the reason why he had postponed or delegated any action to do with the claim.

One major disadvantage to McGuire's researches was that all the information came through Patricia, who had had ample time since 1967 both to verify the facts and to fill in the salient gaps in her father's tale. Despite her apparent openness McGuire was suspicious of her constant disavowals of having anything to gain. If she was so disinterested, why was she making such an enormous effort? And if she was so confident in her father's story, why did she seem to be sustaining its mystery? If she wanted all the details investigated, she was very guarded about the information she gave out. McGuire felt this could only be because she was aware of certain flaws which, even allowing for her father's old age and failing memory, could never have been true. For instance, Maurice Francis had claimed that he and Lord Desmond had been involved for a short time in the Black and Tans – but this paramilitary organization, recruited by the British in Ireland from convicts and other undesirables, had only come into existence many years after Lord Desmond's death. Even more significant was the statement that he had been designated Marquess of Kildare on the death of the fifth Duke in 1893.

Marquess of Kildare is the courtesy title belonging to heirs apparent (that is, eldest sons) of Dukes of Leinster. According to peerage law, Maurice Francis, as second son, would have been heir presumptive, or next in line after his elder brother. He could still have masqueraded as the Duke in public to fulfil the role of a real, invalid Duke; but his succession depended on the sixth Duke not having a son. Even though he assumed this could not happen, as a brother of the Duke he could only be designated Lord Maurice FitzGerald.

Thirdly, there were some notable omissions in Maurice Francis' description of the Coronation in 1902. The ceremony, scheduled for 6 June, was postponed at the last minute because the King was stricken with appendicitis, and when it did take place seven weeks later it was an unrehearsed shambles. The octogenarian Archbishop of Canterbury trickled some of the sacred oil down the Queen's nose while anointing her, and had leaned heavily on the King for support throughout the service. After the ceremony the imperious Duchess of Devonshire had been so eager to leave the Abbey in the wake of the royal procession that she plunged headlong down the steps, her coronet falling from her head. Maurice had failed to mention any of these incidents which had provided topics of conversation for weeks. Instead, he spoke of long rehearsals and described how he raised his coronet as he knelt before the King – but only the peers and their wives raised their coronets; the pages did not even carry them. McGuire felt that such an inaccurate account indicated only that he could not have been there. A photograph would settle the matter, but McGuire was unable to obtain one, and a drawing of Edward VII's train-bearers which he found in a contemporary copy of the *Illustrated London News* did not show the Duke of Leinster's face as clearly as a photograph might.

And, finally, what of the 'abdication agreement' itself? The sixth Duke had evidently disappeared after 1910. According to Maurice Francis, this was when he had come to America; the man who died in 1922 was the elder brother. But why had Lord Edward pressed for the title so strongly? By inheriting the dukedom Lord Edward, far from gaining anything, stood to lose everything because of the deal he had made in 1920.

Whatever the truth in Maurice Francis' story, there was no doubt in McGuire's mind that the circumstances surrounding the death of the sixth Duke were peculiar. There had been no announcement in *The Times* until four days after it had taken place, and the date given was 4 February 1922, not 2 February. There had been no mention of a funeral, and no death certificate had so far been located. All he had from Patricia was the 'registered information' provided by the Duke's next of kin, Lord Frederick FitzGerald, an uncle, who gave the causes of death as 'pneumonia ($4\frac{1}{2}$ days) and epilepsy (25 years)'.

According to Brian Masters' book, the Duke had been suffering from a brain tumour, and this could explain the lack of information about the sixth Duke after 1910. He presumably spent the rest of his life in the Edinburgh sanatorium, and never went about in public. But would Lord Edward have entered into his agreement with Mallaby-Deeley if his elder brother were an invalid and not expected to live long? Whether Maurice Francis was lying or not it seemed that something out of the ordinary had happened to the real Duke which the family had been at pains to conceal.

McGuire was furious with himself for not following up the 1967 obituary sooner, as he had intended, especially as the one man who might have been able to settle the matter of the 'abdication', the seventh Duke, was now dead.

With the death of the seventh Duke, Leonard's claim to the dukedom became public – and, hardly surprisingly, his story found immediate interest with the press. A stringer for the *News of the World* began investigations in San Francisco. He interviewed Leonard and Patricia and was then referred to McGuire. Though he was anxious to point out that the results of his research were purely circumstantial, McGuire passed on all he knew. On 19 August 1976 the outline of the story arrived by telex at the London office of the *News of the World*. It was fascinating, but the newspaper could not publish anything until it was checked for feasibility and plausibility. For such purposes they often used a freelance agent called John Ford, a specialist in legal and historical investigation. Ford was aware of the importance of the freelance agent to newspapers which were constantly pressed by deadlines and libel actions; he had built up an unchallenged reputation in his profession and felt secure in the knowledge that after 1900 there were few facts which could not be substantiated, few documents which could not be unearthed, few people who could not be traced.

But when he opened the large envelope from the *News of the World* he little knew that its contents were to monopolize his life for the following two years. From the telex he learned that a Californian named Leonard FitzGerald was laying claim to the dukedom of Leinster, made vacant in March by the death of the seventh Duke. His story, based on what his father had told him, was that the seventh Duke's predecessor and elder brother had not died, as publicly reported, in Edinburgh in 1922. Instead, Leonard's father, Maurice Francis FitzGerald, had 'abdicated' in favour of his younger brother so that he could escape the family and start a new life in America. Such an arrangement, the claimant said, should not be allowed to prevent his own claim being recognized, even at this late date, since it had no legal validity. There were, however, two problems. Firstly, other than the stories he had been told, he had no evidence by which his father's bona fides could be established, and, secondly, the story of the abdication was not as straightforward as it appeared. Leonard maintained that his father

47

had not himself been the rightful holder of the title sixth Duke of Leinster; there had been an elder brother of whose existence there was no record. An invalid from birth, he had been unable to fulfil the required ducal functions, and the latter had there-fore devolved on Maurice, the second son. Many of the details of the story had been confirmed through the efforts of a San Franciscan named McGuire, but the existence of an invalid elder brother – whose name, according to Leonard's father, was Frederick – was still not proven. The telex went on to discuss much about the life of Maurice Francis FitzGerald; it related McGuire's discoveries, doubts and conclusions. Ford found the wealth of detail confusing. He knew little about the peerage, less about the Leinsters, nothing about America. Nevertheless he felt certain that the crucial issue was whether or not there had been a fourth boy. Instinct told him that the best point at which to start was the death in 1922, and he went directly to the Public Records Office.

Over the next few days he checked McGuire's research. In almost all respects he found it to be correct. From 11 March 1910, when *The Times* announced 'The Duke of Leinster will shortly arrive in England from abroad', until 6 February 1922, when it announced that he had died two days earlier, there was not a single reference to the activities or whereabouts of the sixth Duke in that newspaper. Ford could not find any mention of a visit to Australia in 1907 – confirmed, according to the telex, by a member of the Duke's family resident there – but he found mention of the Duke travelling there five years earlier. A trip made by the Duke to Egypt in 1909 was confirmed, and so was a reference to a journey to South Africa not mentioned in the telex.

From the authorities in Edinburgh he received a copy of the death certificate of Maurice, Duke of Leinster, dated 2 Febru-ary 1922, which confirmed the causes of death – epilepsy and pneumonia – given in the register. Ford failed to locate any photographs of the sixth Duke; the only extant Coronation photograph showing any of the pages – to which he was referred by the Royal Archivist at Windsor – did not show the Duke of Leinster.

The *News of the World*'s brief gave very little time for the job, so Ford gave the paper what he felt to be the only reasonable answer in view of the small amount of research he had been able to complete: the story was indeed feasible and plausible, but this did not make it true. He was pleased when the newspaper decided against publication.

But Ford was still interested, and asked if he could keep the telex and, during whatever spare time he had, looked further into the life of the sixth Duke of Leinster. He tried Tasiemka's newspaper library, a collection of over a million clippings, in case he had a photograph of the sixth Duke, and there found a file of more than ninety clippings on the Leinster family dating back to the late nineteenth century. It included two photographs of the sixth Duke.

One of these had been taken when he was no more than eight, the other at the time of the Coronation while the subject was still at Eton. The latter photograph, a head and shoulders, showed a fair, handsome boy with prominent ears. At this point Ford had no photographs of Maurice Francis FitzGerald with which to compare it. However, he was by now irrevocably involved in the case, and began to set in motion a massive investigative campaign.

But as John Ford made his first major find in the Tasiemka library Leonard FitzGerald received a letter from his solicitors which angered and depressed him. He had already been disappointed when his solicitors had been unable to trace any fingerprints of the sixth Duke, making those taken on his father's death useless. Then the Marquess of Kildare had

49

denied that there was any truth in Maurice's story. Now, in the latest letter, it emerged that the sixth Duke had suffered not from epilepsy or pneumonia, nor a brain tumour, but had been a madman. The House of Lords had found what they claimed to be irrefutable proof – two court orders, one dated 1909 certifying the Duke insane and placing his affairs in the hands of others, and a second, dated 11 April 1919, allowing the Duke's trustees to make a settlement on his behalf. Not surprisingly, Leonard now felt certain that his father was the victim of a conspiracy: 11 April 1919 was the day before Maurice Francis' first marriage.

Nevertheless, Leonard decided to withdraw his claim. Increasingly worried about his health and the exorbitant expense of employing a solicitor – he had already spent about ten thousand dollars – he saw no alternative. He was more convinced than ever of the truth of his father's story; there was no doubt in his mind that between the Leinsters and the Mallaby-Deeleys a thorough cover-up had been perpetrated. Whereas the House of Lords saw the court order of 11 April 1919 as definite proof that the Duke was in England, Leonard saw it as an indication that the FitzGeralds would go to any lengths to conceal his father's escape. It wasn't difficult to find a reason for this, for Lord Edward had first entered into his agreement with Mallaby-Deeley in 1918 and before it could be finalized in September 1920 any trace of fraudulence would have to be removed.

Leonard received his solicitor's letter in mid August 1976. Although the House of Lords had given him until the end of September to produce evidence supporting his case he saw little point in delaying the Writ of Summons for the Marquess of Kildare. In spite of receiving no response to a friendly letter of introduction he had written a few months earlier he felt no bitterness towards the Marquess.

When interviewed by the *News of the World* he said: 'There's not a dime in this for me, but I am recovering from a massive heart attack and before I die I would like to know who I am . . . I mean no harm to the man now claiming the title but two questions must be answered. Who was my father? And what rights does my ten-year-old son have?' For, if Leonard's father was not Maurice, sixth Duke of Leinster, who was he?

4

Crossed Lines

NOW that Leonard had withdrawn his claim the burden of finding proof lay on Patricia's shoulders. She needed someone to help her, and made a further visit to London, ostensibly on holiday. There she contacted John Ford, whose appetite was already whetted for more information on the FitzGerald claimant. Ford was just as anxious as Patricia to pursue investigations, but he wasn't at all sure he would come up with the answers she wanted, for even before they met he had serious doubts about her father's story. He had learned a great deal about the life of the seventh Duke. He had been in touch with McGuire, who had told him about the inaccuracies in Maurice Francis' description of the Coronation and the impossibility of his being designated Marquess of Kildare in 1893. But Ford's doubts were mainly founded on certain important inconsistencies in the story itself.

When Ford had first read the telex he felt that the most important factor was the 'fourth child'. Now he received details from Patricia of the earlier discussions with Dermot Morrah of the claim which made no mention whatsoever of such a child. At Ford's meeting with Patricia, she took pains to emphasize that her father had only ever claimed to be rightful Duke of

Leinster *after* 1922, a clear indication that Maurice Francis was the second son and that the eldest, Frederick, had indeed died in 1922. But if, as Patricia said, this was so, it made the story of the abdication in January nonsensical – unless it was certain that Frederick was about to die or was already dead. But the 1922 death certificate gave no indication of any such slow and predictable demise with its 'pneumonia (4½ days)'. Moreover it was quite clear from a memorandum Morrah prepared on Leonard's claim that he had been told nothing of any elder boy. Outside Patricia's reconstructions and transcriptions of her father's memories the only time a fourth boy was specifically mentioned was in the letter Leonard had written to the Marquess of Kildare in 1976, and even then it betrayed Leonard's doubts: 'Are you aware of there ever being any one in the family whom my father would have thought to be an elder brother? He often spoke of this person whose name seemed to have been Frederick. There were so many in the household I cannot imagine to whom he was referring. Some of the family and those acquainted with the Leinsters at that time have also referred to "Frederick".' Leonard didn't name these sources, but it wasn't surprising that a Frederick should have been spoken of, since one of the guardians of the fifth Duke's children was his brother, Lord Frederick FitzGerald.

Leonard and his sisters agreed on one thing, that it was in 1913 that their father had come to settle in America. They were also fairly sure that he had visited the country one or more times before that. According to a letter from the United States Immigration and Naturalization Service, it was recorded that one Francis FitzGerald had entered America on 7 January 1919. This man, undoubtedly their father, had said at the time that he was a farmer aged thirty-one, born near Dublin, and that he had resided previously in the United States in New York in 1907 and in Montana from 1912 to 1915. The letter also said that he had been admitted to Canada in 1905 on the ss *Victorian*.

Patricia did not tell Ford everything at their first meeting; she felt it was asking too much to hear the tapes of her father talking, but she agreed to send him transcripts of anything she considered important. She said she didn't want anyone, even her own brother, hearing some of the terrible things their father had said about his family. Ford was alarmed to hear that Patricia would effectively monitor any evidence deriving from her father's memories on tape, but hoped that the information he needed could be found in the archives of newspapers and magazines.

Ford badly needed photographs for identification. Having seen photographs of Patricia's father which she brought with her he knew the ones he had found in Tasiemka's library were not of Maurice Francis. But he now had a clipping from the *Winnipeg Free Press Prairie Farmer* of 13 August 1922 which Maurice Francis had left among his possessions. Under a photograph of a moustachioed young man appeared the caption: 'Duke of Leinster. Irish nobleman who is joining the Free State Army to aid in restoring peace to Ireland.' Except in the shape of the ear, the subject little resembled the fair-haired youth at the time of the Coronation in 1902. But who then was he? Certainly not Patricia's father, nor the seventh Duke (who had succeeded to the title seven months earlier), nor Frederick, for even if he had existed he was, according to Maurice Francis, dead by February 1922. And if it was simply Maurice, sixth Duke of Leinster, what was he doing joining the army six months after he was supposed to be dead?

The events with which Ford was concerned had taken place several decades before. The two signatories to the 'abdication agreement' were both dead. If such an agreement had existed it would in any case have been a well kept secret. Nevertheless

Ford decided to try every possibility, and on 20 October he advertiseed in *The Times* asking anyone who had known the Leinster boys to contact him.

Meanwhile, McGuire was pursuing his investigations in America, where he was becoming increasingly aware of the fact that without Leonard's claim no one would have thought to investigate the life of the sixth Duke of Leinster. No doubt this was partly because the seventh Duke's excesses had provided a smoke screen, drawing attention away from his brother. All the same, it was odd no one had questioned the circumstances surrounding his death at that time, as the fortunes of the family depended so greatly on his remaining alive.

Like Ford, McGuire recognized that Patricia had provided two distinct versions of her father's story. The first – told to Dermot Morrah shortly after her father's death – was that her father was Maurice, Duke of Leinster, the eldest of three brothers, who had run away to America, made an agreement in January 1922 with Lord Edward FitzGerald in Montreal by which he abdicated the title, and that after this a false report of his death was made. The second – told to McGuire and Ford – was that her father was the second of four brothers, the eldest boy being an invalid whose existence was kept from the world, and that because of this the ducal duties had devolved on Maurice, who had later run away to America; in February 1922 the invalid boy had died and Maurice had 'abdicated'. Maurice's death was announced in his place, and Maurice remained in America. Each story was far-fetched, each full of holes.

Whether the Californian was an imposter or not, McGuire was still perplexed by what had happened to the sixth Duke. If he was an epileptic, why was their talk of 'incurable imbecility' and a brain tumour? If the Duke had been certified insane, where had he lived? Leonard's solicitors said they had found no medical records at Craighouse in his name after 1913.

When Ford sent McGuire the *Illustrated London News* drawing of the train-bearers at the Coronation McGuire's doubts were confirmed. The train-bearer Duke and Maurice Francis were not the same person, but the train-bearer Duke and the subject of the photograph in Tasiemka's library were.

McGuire also found that on the subject of the Duke the American press was so consistently misleading that it was as if the errors were deliberate. McGuire had only two official documents to date: death certificates for Maurice Francis FitzGerald and for Maurice FitzGerald, Duke of Leinster, on both of which the same parents and dates of birth were given. To these he could add two American obituaries of the sixth Duke and three articles on him which had appeared in New York newspapers between 1905 and 1922. He was surprised to find that the *New York Times'* obituary had announced the Duke's death on 5 February 1922, one day before the London *Times*. He was perplexed by the *San Francisco Examiner* obituary dated 25 February 1922 which said the Duke had visited the United States twice:

From the time he attained his majority, in 1908, until his death, the press of the Empire and America was filled with rumours and conjectures of probable romances and possible marriages ... of the young Duke ... [who] was said to be the handsomest peer in the Empire ... Owing to his delicate health, the young duke, known for his small stature as 'the little duke', spent several years travelling about the world under the care of a tutor, and during that time covered much of the western portion of the United States. This tour was made incognito, but after the duke visited New York officially, and during this time the

57

rumour became current that he was to wed an American
girl ... the new duke is only thirty years old and shares
the delicate constitution which was the heritage of his
brother.

McGuire could find no evidence that any such American
tour had in fact taken place; shipping records for that period
are incomplete or lost. The *New York Times'* index made no
reference to any visit to America, although one appears to have
been planned. The morgue at the *New York Times* contained a
clipping from the *New York Daily Tribune* of 18 December 1905
which declared: 'Young Duke of Leinster Coming to This
Country':

The Duke of Leinster, having now attained his eighteenth
year, has left Eton ... and is about to undertake a trip
around the world, coming first to America, where he will
spend several months before going on to China and Japan,
returning home by India. Australia he has already visited,
making the trip to the Antipodes four years ago for the
sake of the sea voyage ordered by his doctors. Until a year
or two ago he was exceedingly delicate, and grave fears
were entertained that he would fall a prey to that dread
malady which has been named the 'white plague' –
namely, consumption – to which both his father and lovely
mother, one of the most famous and popular beauties of
her day, succumbed. But he has outgrown the danger and
has developed into a tall, healthy, handsome lad, who,
moreover, when he attains his majority, three years hence,
will find himself in possession of a large fortune, the family
property having been carefully nursed and wisely
administered during his long minority, while the Irish
Land Act has afforded to the trustees opportunities for

making the most advantageous sales of his superfluous and unproductive lands in Ireland.

In another New York newspaper, the *Evening Sun* of 11 September 1919, McGuire found another long piece about the sixth Duke written by the gossip columnist known as the Marquise de Fontenoy.

That Ireland's premier peer, the now thirty-two year old Duke of Leinster, head of the historic house of FitzGerald, has been under restraint for the last two years as a confirmed and incurable imbecile, was, although, long known in certain circles, first made public the other day during the course of an examination of his only surviving brother and heir, Lord Edward FitzGerald, in bankruptcy proceedings.

Both his father, the fifth Duke, and his mother, the greatest beauty of her day, succumbed at short intervals from one another to consumption, and it seems that the same fell malady, namely, tuberculosis, has attacked their eldest son, the present Duke, fastening itself not upon his lungs but upon his brain.

The young Duke was in his boyhood in very delicate health and did not remain long at Eton, whither he had been sent after leaving the school which the clergyman Marquis of Normanby was wont to maintain in Mulgrave Castle, his ancestral home in Yorkshire. In fact the Duke left Eton in order to take a number of sea voyages on specially chartered yachts under the care of relatives and physicians.

It was during one of these cruises that he landed at New Orleans, and tried in turn the dry air of the Texas plains, the pine lands of the Mississippi and the mountain air of

Colorado. He dropped his title when travelling and spent more than a year in the United States without attracting attention.

By the time the Duke had come of age, he was a sturdy stripling, over six feet in height, able to take part in athletics and in sports on the field and in the water. Indeed while at Oxford, it seemed as if he had entirely outgrown the danger of tuberculosis with which he had been threatened by heredity. And then all of a sudden the fell disease attacked his brain and for the last three years he has been in a sanatorium awaiting death as a release, his case being quite incurable.

He is ignorant therefore of the fact that his favourite brother, Lord Desmond, fell in the war, and that his youngest brother and heir, Lord Edward FitzGerald, who was invalided back from France with a wound, and with a pension from the War Department of $500 a year, has, after marrying May Etheridge, a London comedy actress, been making ducks and drakes of his expected inheritance and of eventual rights to the entailed possessions of the dukedom.

McGuire found two further references to the seventh Duke which had some bearing on his research. One was from the *New York Sun* in February 1922 which stated that the sixth Duke had died the previous week from tuberculosis 'after having the last two years of his somewhat pathetic existence darkened by imbecility'. Apropos his successor, the article continued: 'After leaving the army he spent some time travelling in the US and Canada where he purchased several hundred town lots of land in northern Alberta which possibly escaped his creditors.' Also referring to the seventh Duke, the *Edmonton Journal* of 8 April 1922 said: 'In 1908 . . . when he was twenty-one he made a tour of the US and Canada accompanied by a tutor. He travelled incognito under the name of Maurice FitzGerald and discouraged all attempts to make a fuss over him.' Perhaps the latter reference was lifted from an earlier American article, for it can only have referred to the sixth Duke. At the same time, if the trip had been made in secret how did so many newspapers come to hear of it? Was it possible that the source was not the American press at all but a certain expatriate coincidentally living in Edmonton in 1922 under the name of Maurice Francis FitzGerald? The same notion might easily apply to the photograph and caption in the *Winnipeg Free Press Prairie Farmer* published in August 1922: why else should that newspaper, and no other, print such a curious announcement below a picture clearly not of the seventh Duke? McGuire did not know whether the seventh Duke had purchased any land in Canada, but he knew perfectly well who did own land in Alberta at that time.

If Maurice Francis was an imposter, McGuire had now to face a deceit which had been planned more than half a century before the perpetrator died. Patricia's father had definitely taken the name 'Francis FitzGerald' as early as June 1916, immediately after the death of someone who might have been a key witness – Lord Desmond, Maurice Francis' 'beloved brother'. Whatever else could be deduced from Maurice Francis' story, it was clear that he must have been privy to a wealth of information not generally known about the Leinster family.

But none of this helped McGuire's quest for information about the man who was said to have died in Craighouse on the morning of 2 February 1922, except that by September 1919 he was known to be an 'incurable imbecile'. The Scottish Health Service Central Legal Office sent McGuire a photocopy of the medical report for the five days up to that date, which was verified by a doctor. The details appeared to be correct, but this did not preclude their being faked. The two typewritten sheets described an attack of pneumonia, the treatment provided, the progress of the illness and the patient's death. No indication was given of either insanity or epilepsy. The entire record of the five days had been typed up after the patient's supposed death, his age being given as thirty-four rather than thirty-five, the age on the death certificate; the top half of the first sheet had been carefully blanked out. Why the patient's age should have been changed, McGuire did not know; if he was born on 1 March 1887 he would have been thirty-four and eleven months. At any rate, it was clear that the patient had been in Craighouse before the onset of the illness which apparently killed him.

McGuire made a list of questions, and with these by his side telephoned Craighouse towards the end of October 1976. He hoped to catch the authorities off guard. In this he was more successful than he had hoped, for the health service solicitor whom he rang actually had the sixth Duke's file open on his desk. This extraordinary coincidence may have had something to do with various British newspaper articles appearing at that time.

According to the solicitor, the inmate known as the sixth Duke of Leinster – a handsome, fair-haired, pleasant, well-nourished young man, over six feet in height and weighing fifteen stone – had been admitted to Craighouse on 17 June 1909. He had been brought, bound and tied, by servants. From that day he never left Craighouse, though he was aware that during the ensuing years it was being given out in the press that he was elsewhere. He became extremely violent when he read in the *Gentlewoman's Magazine* of 24 July 1919 that 'the thirty-two-year-old Duke of Leinster leads a quiet life in Ireland'. There were several examples of the Duke's troublesome behaviour in the records, but the solicitor did not think these should be revealed to McGuire. He was at pains to stress that the patient wasn't always ill; the record for one day in May 1913 described him as 'very well, in extremely good humour, having the usual number of fits'. The solicitor denied that the inmate suffered from tuberculosis or a tumour on the brain. There were no references to any visitors and no entries whatsoever for the three occasions after 1909 on which the sixth Duke had signed codicils to his will. That the Duke had signed these demanded his being at least of testamentary capacity. The file did not say who claimed or removed the body of the Duke after his death, but McGuire knew that his uncle, Lord Frederick, must have hurried over from Ireland in order to have registered the death on the same day it occurred.

The solicitor said there were no photographs or fingerprints of the inmate. However, he added that the inmate had written a letter to a Mr Clyde on 9 February 1912 and that he would send a photocopy to McGuire. The letter read in part: 'I live under an assumed name, that of my family, namely Mr FitzGerald, in reality being by birth the head of the family and owning the dukedom of Leinster and other titles'. That the letter hadn't been sent to Mr Clyde perhaps suggested that someone was attempting to keep the inmate's whereabouts secret. Although the letter showed that the inmate imagined himself to be the Duke of Leinster there was no evidence proving the inmate was the Duke – except that the file said so. The inmate's fury on reading that the Duke of Leinster was living quietly in Ireland suggested either that someone was acting his part or that he was being concealed against his will.

McGuire was surprised to learn that the inmate had received no visitors. The seventh Duke, who had every reason to hope that his elder brother would live for many years, had apparently not bothered to see him either before or after his protracted negotiations with Mallaby-Deeley. Moreover, it was highly unlikely that Mallaby-Deeley would have entered into the agreement without first-hand knowledge of the sixth Duke's condition. It was undoubtedly convenient that the sixth Duke died less than two years after Mallaby-Deeley had settled Edward's debts. But then, if he had not expected the sixth Duke to die fairly soon what other reasons could he have had for making such an offer?

5

Press Cuttings

FORD had been the first to admit that he didn't expect much from advertising, so he was surprised to read an article about the FitzGeralds in the *Scotsman* which appeared the day after his advertisement in *The Times*. The article referred to the eighth Duke of Leinster as being the 'wrong person' to sit in the House of Lords, and said that investigations were being undertaken at Craighouse to clarify the issue. The suggestions made in the article coincided with a letter which Leonard FitzGerald had recently received, two months after giving up his claim, and which he passed on to Ford.

The letter was on House of Lords writing-paper and signed 'A Peer of the Realm'. It told Leonard that he was unquestionably the genuine Duke, that the seventh Duke had known this perfectly well, that he had been in touch with the Californian (Leonard's father) several times and had received a deathbed message sent via an Irish priest. The letter went on to say that the seventh Duke's widow, Vivien, Dowager Duchess of Leinster, knew all this but had been persuaded to keep quiet about it ('having been bought off' the letter said) and that 'in spite of her silence she is unhappy and disturbed, because she knows your claim to be just'. At the end of the letter, after exhorting Leonard to come to London without delay, the author asked him to send the Dowager Duchess and Sir Denis Dobson, Clerk of the Crown, whatever 'documentary proof, correspondence and photographs' he possessed. It later turned out that a similar letter was sent to Leonard's solicitors in London; it was dated the same day but was typed on a different machine.

Before Ford could make contact with Vivien he was distracted by an article in *The Observer* of 24 October with the headline 'I'm a Duke, Says the Teacher'. It turned out that the author of the piece, Michael Davie, had seen Ford's advertisement four days earlier, and 'entirely sceptical' had contacted Leonard direct. He was referred to Patricia, who gave him a brief outline of her father's story. Michael Davie then spoke to the eighth Duke, but was told he refused to discuss family matters either with the press or with Leonard's solicitors.

Michael Davie gave a succinct account of the history and role of the FitzGeralds, the life and gambles of the seventh Duke, Leonard's claim and the steps he might take were he able to come up with corroboration for it. The weakness of the story, Davie concluded, was that if Maurice had run away how could his uncles have been sure that he would not return eventually to reassume his inheritance, leaving them to explain the inmate of the asylum?

Davie and Ford had a discussion the following week which formed the substance of a further article in *The Observer* of 3 October 1976. The real significance of the two articles, the first clear explanation of Leonard's claim in the English press, was to generate the public response which Ford's advertisement had failed to do. Unfortunately Davie was tempted to append his own most convincing theory to the second article, assuming without foundation that Maurice Francis FitzGerald, or whoever he was, had genuine connections with the Leinster FitzGeralds.

The most plausible theory I can construct runs as follows. Maurice [Francis], though brought up as the sixth Duke, was illegitimate; his father was someone other than the fifth Duke. The mad boy was another son, a mongol perhaps, the birth was never announced. After the parents' deaths, when Maurice was coming of age, the uncles told him he had no legal right to inherit. To hush up the scandal, they arranged for the mad son to be committed in Maurice's name. The well-known doctor [Pollock] was hired to reassure inquirers that Maurice's apparently sudden lunacy was getting proper medical attention; the committal had to be managed outside the family circle. The Californian Maurice could not return and claim the title without facing up to the doubts about his parents' marriage and his own legitimacy. But he was anxious to preserve his children's claim, possibly in the belief that they could stake a claim without its fundamental illegitimacy coming to light.

This conclusion was confounded by a series of letters which arrived during the next few days.

Mr David Matthews wrote enclosing a photograph of the sixth Duke of Leinster which had appeared in the June 1905 issue of the *Lady's Realm*. It showed a stout boy with close-cropped hair wearing a short jacket, Eton collar and boots tied to the knee; he bore no resemblance to Maurice Francis or to the photograph of the Duke which appeared at the time of the Coronation, except perhaps in the shape of the ears. Beside the photograph was a paragraph about the Duke, describing his delicacy and that he had to leave Eton soon after his arrival there in order to travel for his health.

Another letter came from Dr Marie Boylan, whose father was the doctor in Maynooth.

We were not of course on social terms – in fact there was no such thing, as only Lord Frederick was in residence at Carton. I remember the Duke's coming of age, Lord Desmond being killed in France and some of the exploits of the late Duke [Edward]. The Duke [Maurice] used to visit Carton occasionally accompanied by an attendant. He was definitely insane. My father was invited to visit him, as a matter of courtesy, I suppose. . . .

A far more significant letter came from Sir James Corry, Bt, who remembered the sixth Duke at Eton. He had also attended Mulgrave Castle School, Whitby, Yorkshire, shortly after the Duke had left, and where people remembered him well. Later Corry had lived in the Cromwell Road, London, and had seen a good deal of his aunt, a Mrs Clark who lived at 255 Earl's Court Road, directly opposite the house occupied by Dr Pollock. Pollock was a good friend of the Clarks, and looked after Corry's 'boyish ailments'. One day – Corry wasn't sure exactly when, but before 1912 – he had called upon Pollock and met Maurice, Duke of Leinster there.

> The story as I remember it was that Dr Pollock was found to have a good influence on the Duke (epilepsy?) and was given a handsome salary and the promise of a lump sum eventually, if he would give up his practice and devote all his time to the Duke. This carried on for a few years but the Duke's condition deteriorated in such a manner that he had to be put into a mental institution.

Corry then went on to say that his father had met a friend, a yacht broker, at his club one day. As far as Corry could remember, the friend had said: 'You know something about the Duke of Leinster: I have a peculiar problem. A steam yacht was chartered and is already at Cannes (?) to take the Duke on a

Mediterranean cruise, but no one has turned up and I haven't heard a word.' Corry remembered it being thought that the Duke would benefit from the adventure but he apparently took a bad turn and in the confusion his family entirely forgot about the plan for a cruise. However, Corry was the only person to come forward who knew Dr Pollock well. He wrote:

> Dr Pollock had trained as an engineer before he took up medicine, and (as you see in *Who's Who*) he did not take up medical practice again after his duty to the Duke came to an end ... His entry in *Who's Who* is an indication that the sixth Duke did not go to America a normal and fit person when the American Claimant said he did. I saw Sir Donald Pollock subsequently. He had come south to London and looked in at my office to see me. I mention this to show that he was a family friend as well as medical adviser.

Pollock's career was a very distinguished one but the *Who's Who* entry concerning him was perplexing. When his first biographical entry appeared in 1937 it stated that he was 'General adviser and personal physician to the late Duke of Leinster 1907–12'; ten years later the dates had been amended to read '1907–21', and in 1957 it read '1907–26', four years after the Duke's supposed death.

James Arthur, a Fellow of the Scottish Society of Antiquaries and a general practitioner, would have gladly forsaken his medical career for the dusty world of archives and parish records if only he had had the resources. It was his obsession with tales of aristocratic intrigue which prompted him to write direct to Leonard FitzGerald when he read of his claim in the *Scotsman* and *The Observer*, and offer his assistance in unmasking the rogue Duke of Leinster. James Arthur's sympathies lay unmistakably with the underdog. Leonard had replied, welcoming his support, and suggesting he contact Ford.

After hearing from Ford, James Arthur visited the British Newspaper Library at Colindale which contains numerous Irish newspapers and magazines. (McGuire had only referred to *The Times*, one of the very few newspapers to publish an index, when checking Maurice Francis' story.) With only the vaguest idea of what to look for James Arthur scrutinized hundreds of issues of the *Irish Society and Social Review* and *Kildare Observer* which could be relied upon to print something about the FitzGeralds on even the most trivial occasions. They even printed full lists of passengers arriving on the boat from England.

Contrary to Maurice Francis' asseverations, the sixth Duke had not been in Ireland for his coming of age celebrations (though, if Maurice Francis were himself not the Duke, he might well have been there). According to the *Kildare Observer* of 7 March 1908 the Athy District Council had been told that the Duke 'would be pleased to receive an address from the Council at his present address, 140 Earls Court Road, London'. It was clear from the minutes of the council meeting that the Duke was absent on account of his health. 'It was with feelings of very great regret', reported the paper, 'that the people of the district heard of his protracted illness.' No hint of precisely what ailed the Duke was given in the *Irish Society and Social Review* of the same date. On the contrary:

> The twenty-first birthday of the Duke of Leinster which fell on Sunday was an occasion of quite particular happiness and more than usual cordial congratulations in the large and affectionate family circle in which he is the central object of interest.

There was no more pathetic little figure some thirteen

years ago than that of the eight-year-old head of the FitzGeralds.

His lovely mother, born Lady Hermione Duncombe, had just followed her husband to the grave in the prime of her womanly beauty, leaving three little orphaned boys.

And the pathos of the situation was increased by the fact that the constitution of the little Duke was at that time, and for some years afterwards, so alarmingly delicate as to cause continual anxiety to his relatives.

The Duke was sent, at the usual age, to Eton, where his good looks and pleasant manners made him popular with his companions.

But his education was much interrupted by his delicate health. On account of this he was sent on several lengthy voyages to the Antipodes and to South Africa.

He afterwards resided with a tutor at Oxford with a view to entering the University. But he did not in fact matriculate.

Everyone is glad to know that he has in very great measure outgrown his boyish delicacy. He is now a fairly strong youth, fully six feet in height, and gifted with an engaging personality, and frank, courteous address.

These gifts make him very well liked among his own people round Carton, his home in Kildare.

After a description of Carton, the article went on:

The Duke has another place in County Kildare besides Carton, namely, Kilkea Castle, which is the residence of his bachelor uncle, Lord Walter FitzGerald, and his three aunts, the Ladies Eva, Mabel, and Nesta FitzGerald.

Lady Nesta accompanied her nephew five years ago on his voyage to South Africa and back.

Another of his uncles, Lord Charles, who is married to a

lady of Greek family, has lived in Victoria for some years. The Duke stayed with him when he visited Australia in 1902.

One of His Grace's hobbies is trees, and he is much interested in his fine woods in the demesne of Carton.

Although there is no mention of the Duke being ill at the time, 'delicacy' was a contemporary euphemism which tended to refer to a weak chest. Although Maurice Francis may have suffered from this he certainly wasn't 'fully six feet in height'. On his Canadian Overseas Expeditionary Force discharge certificate his height was correctly given as five feet ten inches.

Other newspapers made it clear that the sixth Duke was and remained, in poor health for at least the next two years, 1908 to 1910, though none stated the exact complaint. The *Carlow Sentinel* of 10 July 1909 announced: 'The Duke of Leinster, who has chartered the steam yacht *Larander*, has had to postpone his cruise owing to indisposition.' The same paper, quoting the *Westminster Gazette*, reported on 23 October 1909 that the Duke was suffering 'from some nervous ailment which gives great anxiety to his friends'. All this corroborated Sir James Corry's memories of the cancelled yacht. From the *Irish Society and Social Review* on 6 November 1909: 'The health of the Duke ... gives rise to a good deal of anxiety ... he is now suffering from a nervous malady, and another winter abroad is ordered.' The following spring, the *Carlow Sentinel* announced on 19 March 1910: 'The Duke of Leinster, who entered upon his twenty-fourth year last week has been wintering abroad. Though tall and fairly well built, the Duke is far from strong, and he finds the rigours of the English winter rather too much for him. The Duke has inherited the good looks of his parents, and, unfortunately, their delicate constitutions also.'

On 13 August 1910 the same paper had happier news to

72

report: 'The Duke of Leinster, whose health has long been delicate, is now much better and has been passing some time in Edinburgh, the climate of which suits him very well.' This seemed a rather strange remark to James Arthur, who well knew the effects of Edinburgh's notorious sea fogs – hardly the most bracing tonic for a supposed consumptive. The Duke's stay in Edinburgh was confirmed in the *Kildare Observer* of 15 October 1910, which described Lord Frederick FitzGerald visiting Scotland where his nephew had been 'for the last month'. The article concluded with: 'The Duke, whose health has been far from good for some time, is at present very unwell.' But the following week a most curious retraction was printed, to the effect that the paper 'was pleased to announce that statements which have been published recently regarding the health of the Duke of Leinster are inaccurate. We are asked to state that the Duke is very well, and is enjoying his stay in Scotland.' James Arthur was amazed to see this, and wondered who could have asked the newspaper to make such a statement, and why.

On 11 March 1911 a supplement to the *Kildare Observer* stated that: 'The Duke of Leinster has just celebrated his twenty-fourth birthday. Happily the young Duke's illness last October was not as serious as represented. He is in a delicate state of health and has been compelled to winter abroad for several years.' There were further references to the Duke in the Irish press, but James Arthur couldn't find one which specified his exact whereabouts. This ratified the House of Lords' statement that the sixth Duke was certified insane after 1909, and was presumably being looked after discreetly somewhere in Scotland.

James Arthur found one report which corroborated Maurice Francis' memories of his parents' happy marriage. In the March 1910 issue of the *Irish Society and Social Review* the sixth

Duke's parents were described as 'Being a love-match in every way . . . the menage seemed to be a very happy one . . . in these days of ill-assorted marriages it was refreshing to see a young couple living happily together far from London and its frivolities.' The paper didn't mention that the sixth Duke's parents had in fact been dead for some fifteen years.

6

The First-Born

FORD was somewhat bemused by Maurice Francis' claim that the fifth Duke and Duchess of Leinster had only had boys, for contemporary peerage books referred also to a daughter. The 1890 edition of *Burke's Peerage* stated that there had been a daughter who died in 1888, but Ford discovered that this was not the case.

On 5 February 1886, Hermione, then Marchioness of Kildare, had given birth to a daughter at 6 Carlton House Terrace, the FitzGeralds' London house. The child had died, unnamed, the following day. The Carton cemetery was not consecrated until the death of the fourth Duke in February 1887, and Ford could not find a place of burial for the infant in London.

But if there was confusion surrounding the existence of a daughter, it extended to all the children. The 1887 edition of one peerage book had only one child for the Duke and Duchess of Leinster, entered as 'Gerald, Marquis of Kildare, *b*. in April 1887' when he was in fact called Maurice, and born on 1 March 1887; the infant born in 1886 is not mentioned. In obituaries of the fifth Duke the *Yorkshire Gazette* referred to his 'only son, hitherto the Marquess of Kildare' and *The Times* referred to two sons, Maurice

75

and Desmond. On the death of the Duchess the *Graphic* mentioned only two sons, and the *Yorkshire Gazette* that 'four children were born of the marriage – three sons and a daughter – all of whom are living'. Only the *Illustrated London News* mentioned a daughter who died in infancy; the *Kildare Observer*, which had announced the birth of the girl, never noted her death.

Could it be that the unnamed girl had not died, and that she had in fact been a boy? This idea concurred with Maurice Francis' story and was championed by James Arthur who, as a doctor, had a medical explanation for it. There is a condition which involves the genitals of a male child remaining within the body at birth which can give rise to misapprehensions. It could explain Maurice Francis' assertion that there had been four sons and no daughter, and even the seventh Duke's comment in his memoirs that his brother was unable to have children. If the person who died in 1922 had been born in February 1886 rather than March 1887 it would concur with the age given on the death certificate, thirty-five as opposed to thirty-four, and perhaps explain why the tombstone had no birth date on it at all.

Ford then looked up the will of the fourth Duke, Charles William FitzGerald, who had died in February 1887. The fourth Duke would have known about the child born in 1886, and might have mentioned him or her in his will. Unfortunately there was no trace of the fourth Duke's will or that of his wife as the Principal Registry Will Book in Dublin had been destroyed in the Troubles. Nor was it to be found in Somerset House. According to the file kept there, the fourth Duke's will had been one of a batch of ten sent to the Estate Duty Office on 23 September 1955. The Estate Duty Office said that the will was returned with forty others six days later, the nine wills with which it was sent being returned on 30 September. There was no reason given for its initial transfer. Ford had every Irish

Reseal in Somerset House examined, but it was not to be found. Had this been just one example of bureaucratic inefficiency Ford might have ignored it. But this was not the case, as further investigations rapidly made clear.

Apart from the birth certificate of Maurice, Marquess of Kildare, born on 1 March 1887 at Kilkea Castle, Ford found little on the Duke's early years. The *Illustrated London News* published a photograph of 'our youngest duke' on his succession in December 1893. It showed a small plump child with straight fair hair standing on a grand staircase; he had prominent ears, a straight nose and pale skin, features which were confirmed in another photograph published by the *Graphic*. A further photograph, probably taken two years later, in 1895, showed the three boys: Edward, grinning impishly; Desmond, serious, almost surly; the Duke, smiling, seated on a sofa. The children, it appeared, moved about a lot after being orphaned, from Duncombe Park to Netherby Hall – the Grahams' house – and Carton and Kilkea.

When the young Duke and his brothers were staying with their grandfather at Duncombe Park they narrowly escaped being burnt alive when the wing in which they were sleeping caught fire. Maurice was carried down a ladder wrapped in a wet blanket while huge flames leaped out of the windows. This excitement recalled a much earlier incident involving the first Earl of Kildare who as a baby was inadvertently left behind when the wooden Castle of Woodstock, a fourteenth-century FitzGerald stronghold, went up in flames. When a search was made his room was seen to be nothing but a smoking ruin. Fortunately a large pet ape, normally kept chained up, had broken free in the confusion and was found cradling the missing child in its arms. The Earl later adopted monkeys as the supporters of his coat-of-arms in gratitude to the creature who saved his life.

According to the Marquise de Fontenoy, the New York gossip columnist mainly responsible for releasing news of the FitzGeralds to American readers, the Duke left Mulgrave Castle School in Yorkshire to go to Mr Tabor's at Cheam in 1899. It wasn't unusual for boys to go to Cheam – as Mr Tabor's is now called – for a year prior to Eton. For sons of noble families who had been taught at home until they were about ten years old, a year at Cheam broke them into boarding-school life. There was a FitzGerald tradition of going to the school; Lord Desmond went there for three years. No academic records survive for the Duke either at Cheam or at Mulgrave Castle but when the library at Carton was auctioned in 1949 two books awarded to the Duke at Cheam were bought by the wife of the Archdeacon of Maynooth.

In 1900 the young Duke went to Eton, to the Reverend H. T. Bowlby's house. Although some newspapers said he had to leave soon after, he in fact attended the school for over four years, with interruptions. He was absent for the Lent Half each year, the worst time for schoolboy epidemics and for 'chesty boys'. Despite this he passed his trials and never lost his remove by failing the exams. From the Eton List of summer 1903 the Duke appeared to be half-way up the school in the army class. Ford talked to Dr Patrick Strong, the Keeper of the College Library, who managed to track down an old debating book from Bowlby's house which recorded the Duke's maiden speech, almost certainly in his own handwriting, for the debating society on 8 October 1904. The speech showed the Duke was intelligent and well informed.

Of the names Maurice Francis had mentioned when talking of his school days, George Tyler's family had not been able to help and Johnny Beard was not listed in the Eton Register. Johnny Beard had supposedly been the son of one of the masters at Eton, but no Mr Beard had ever taught there.

78

Maurice Francis had also described being confronted by town bullies as he stepped off the tram at the school gates, though no trams had ever run in Eton and the school, an integral part of the town, has no formal gates of the sort a country school might have.

A contemporary of the Duke's at Eton, W. G. McMinnies, provided the nearest thing to a physical description Ford could find. Though not in the same house as the Duke, McMinnies remembered him as 'a fair-haired boy, say five feet seven inches, plump and rather like an elongated egg. His brother was fair-haired and smaller.' This outline, accompanied by a sketch, little resembled the Duke in the drawing of the King's train-bearers, but it wasn't unlike a photograph of the Duke published in 1901 to celebrate his visit to the Houses of Parliament.

The Duke's regular absences from the school were obviously because of his health, but Dr Strong insisted that his sickness could not have been epilepsy, for no boy would have been admitted to Eton with it. Newspapers naturally assumed it was a chest ailment, common enough at the time, and sea air was the recommended cure.

Ford was surprised that the one trip which received a lot of publicity – the sixth Duke's Australian tour in 1902 – was one which Maurice Francis had not even mentioned. Patricia was adamant that her father had been to Australia in 1907, but could produce no documentary evidence to support this. The Duke had boarded the RMS *Ortona* bound for Melbourne on 31 January 1902, and on 20 February *Vanity Fair* reported: 'The Duke of Leinster, who has not been at all strong lately, has been ordered to go on a long sea voyage for the benefit of his health.' He was accompanied by Mr Herbert Stewart, who would be the Duke's companion and tutor. The *Ortona* docked on 12 March and the Duke was welcomed by the *Melbourne Punch*:

79

Now's your time, girls. A real live duke, premier duke, marquis [*sic*] and earl of Ireland, the very swaggerest aristocrat from the 'ould sod'. True, his grace is only fifteen, and is in the charge of a curate, but as one hopeful Collins Street blocker has already remarked, 'No matter, girls, he'll grow.'

(A 'blocker' was the best sort of Melbourne girl; the 'block' in Collins Street the most fashionable shopping area.)

The Duke didn't stay in Melbourne, but went to see his uncle, Lord Charles FitzGerald, at Riddles Creek, Victoria. Lord Charles had left Ireland in the 1880s and on the boat had met Alice Claudius, an Anglo-Greek; they married in Calcutta and settled in Australia. The only FitzGerald of his generation to marry outside the aristocracy, he dropped his courtesy title in deference to the general Australian feeling that titles were outdated. No written or photographic record remains of the Duke's visit to his uncle. A photograph of the Duke in 'diggers dress' taken outside the North Woah Hawp Company mine in Ballarat was due for publication in one of the Australian illustrated weeklies, but never appeared. The Duke, despite his chest complaint, had been right down the mine. A local paper reported that at the Ballarat Benevolent Institution the Duke left the following compliment in the visitors' book: 'I have never seen anything like this institution before in any country. The order, cleanliness and general arrangements were remarkable – Leinster.' (The visitors' book itself has long since been lost.) In ten years' time the Duke would not be so laudatory about such institutions.

On 17 April the *Melbourne Punch* described the Duke's arrival in Adelaide, where he and his tutor were to be the guests of Lord Tennyson, the Governor. The Australian press had followed the whole tour assiduously, including the Duke's arrest for illegally importing grapes for which crime the fine was waived, until his departure in May. In London, the *Tatler* of 25 June noted that the Duke was currently in Australia, although he should have returned by then for the Coronation ceremony which was due to take place that month.

The Duke must have been pleased at the descriptions of himself which appeared in various journals. The *Sketch* wrote:

> The Duke of Leinster, who came back from Australia to take his place as one of the Sovereign's train-bearers ... can, perhaps, claim to be the best-looking of the little group which composes the modern wearers of the strawberry leaves. He inherits good looks from his lovely mother ... he and his younger brother have had a happy boyhood and youth thanks greatly to the devotion and care of their uncles ... from many points of view he is one of the most interesting of the youthful peers.

John Ford could hardly disagree with this last comment. There was no doubt in his mind that it was not Maurice Francis who had made the trip, but he drew a blank when trying to establish the real identity of the young traveller. In view of the theory of the fourth child, the ages of the Duke on the *Ortona*'s passenger lists are significant: on the journey out he was put at fifteen, which was not surprising since, if he was born on 1 March 1887, he would celebrate his birthday during the voyage. On the return journey, however, his age was given as sixteen. Both ages on the lists correspond with those of the girl born in January 1886. Although James Arthur's theory had first struck him as absurd Ford was beginning to change his mind about the girl, especially when he took into account the sixth Duke's age on the death certificate, the absence of a date of birth on the tombstone, the seventh Duke's references in his memoirs that his brother could not have children, the disappearance of copies of the fourth Duke and Duchess's wills – and now the shipping lists. It was also odd that the girl was never named; the fourth Duchess's last child, who was born and died on the same day, appeared in *Burke's* as Robert. Without a name, finding a burial place was impossible.

Ford had long wanted to meet Vivien, Dowager Duchess of Leinster. The anonymous letter on House of Lords writing-paper Leonard had received suggested that she knew about his father, and she might well at the same time resolve the question of the fourth child. Since her husband's death Vivien had been fully occupied running a charity shop, then she had been very ill, finally she had lost her job. Most of her affairs were handled by a trustee. However, when Ford wrote to her he was pleased to have a warm letter from her by return. A few days after this a message was left at his office suggesting they meet for lunch at the Inn on the Park. When Ford rang to confirm the appointment, the Dowager Duchess denied leaving such a message and asked Ford to come instead to her tiny flat.

Ford arrived at six and stayed until three in the morning. Vivien spoke of the FitzGeralds and her dislike of the way they had treated her husband. She also spoke about her stepson, of how he had got on with the Mallaby-Deeleys and of the fact that she was financially dependent on him. This, together with a robbery of a suitcase containing her late husband's effects from the charity shop, had made her feel resentful towards the family. She seemed depressed, and cultivated an air of secrecy which Ford found bewildering in view of her expressed desire to help unravel the mystery.

Vivien had lived with 'Fitz', as she called the seventh Duke, since 1956, and they had married in 1964. He had told her about all his incredible escapades, his three former wives and financial problems, and there were no secrets between them except one – the subject of his eldest brother. Not surprisingly, this became an object of fascination to Vivien, and she often tried to extract details of the sixth Duke from her husband. He described the sixth Duke as over six feet tall, strong and healthy, definitely not mad. He had never seen his brother having a fit. He had been through public school. Why then was he certified insane only after he came of age, and why incarcerated in Edinburgh when there must have been places in Ireland suitable for him? The vague answers Vivien received were totally unsatisfying, but she did not give up. When she asked about the sixth Duke's love affairs or sexuality, she was always told, 'He couldn't.' Was he impotent, she would ask, but 'Fitz' was adamant: the sixth Duke 'just couldn't'.

Shortly before he died 'Fitz' had airily dismissed Leonard's claim, but a few months earlier, in December 1975, something had happened which made Vivien doubt this. Leonard's sister Patricia had written to Rafaelle, Edward's second wife, enclosing a copy of a letter written by her father some forty years before and which Patricia believed was cardinal evidence for Leonard's claim. The letter was unfinished and unsigned; it had never been posted by Patricia's father, and Ford and McGuire, who had seen the original in America, had not paid much attention to it because of this. Rafaelle sent the copy on to the Marquess of Kildare, who then showed it to his father and current stepmother. Vivien told Ford that she had been amazed by the tone of the letter: it was exactly how 'Fitz' spoke and wrote. The letter was dated 22 July 1931, when Maurice Francis was in the throes of his first divorce.

Dear Ted,
Received your letter, and altho I am always glad to hear from you, regret that you see fit to harp continually on the same subject.

Once again I tell you, and this is final, I have no intention of returning to Ireland and claiming the position you now hold. That is of course for myself, and as far as you personally are concerned you need have no fear of me butting in. As for the rights of my little boy, that of course is a different matter, and inspite of the cloud of illegitamcy [*sic*] to which you refer, I shall in due course have that removed.

If I cannot do this through the Courts in Arizona I shall of necessity do so through the Irish Free State. But as you know that will bring our family in the limelight once more and god knows you have done all that is necessary in that line.

I fully understand your wish regarding your own son but surely after all I have done to efface myself and leave you to enjoy what is rightfully mine you cannot in fairness expect me to stand by and see my own child deprived of his rights. Don't forget, so far as I am concerned my marriage was perfectly legal and I had no knowledge of his Mother's duplicity, and I am now taking this matter before the Courts in Arizona which I understand recognizes the legitimacy of the Children.

As far as you and I are concerned there is little to choose from; we have both made a mess of things and neither of us are much credit to the family name.

I have given you ample evidence of my personal feelings towards you, and still being a sentimental idiot, the memory of our boyhood regard for each other is always with me, and I never could have you get out and rustle like I have had to do at times for a sure existence. Anyway I am used to it and you are not. I refuse to accept a penny for myself under the conditions you mention. Dad was not the only FitzGerald with pride and I hope to prove it. But why

Carton, the family seat of the Dukes of Leinster.

Hermione, Duchess of Leinster.

Hermione, Duchess of Leinster with two of her children, Lord Desmond
FitzGerald (left) and the Marquess of Kildare (centre).

The drawing-room at Carton in the 1890s.

Maurice, sixth Duke of
Leinster, dressed as a
train-bearer for the
Coronation of Edward VII.

Craighouse, Edinburgh.

Charles William, fourth Duke of Leinster.

His fifth son, Lord Charles FitzGerald, in the 1880s.

Maurice FitzGerald of California.

Bandmaster Tyler in 1901.

The Bandmaster, Maurice FitzGerald (standing), Frederick and Nin Tyler during the First World War.

Captain Lord Desmond FitzGerald
shortly before his death in 1916.

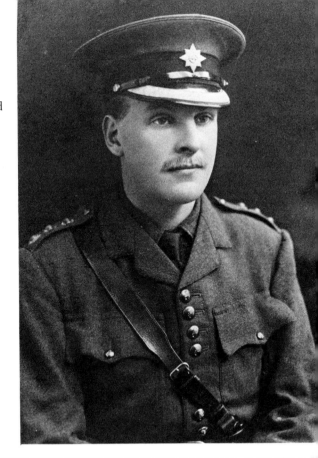

Vivien, Duchess of Leinster
helping Edward, the seventh
Duke, with his coronet.

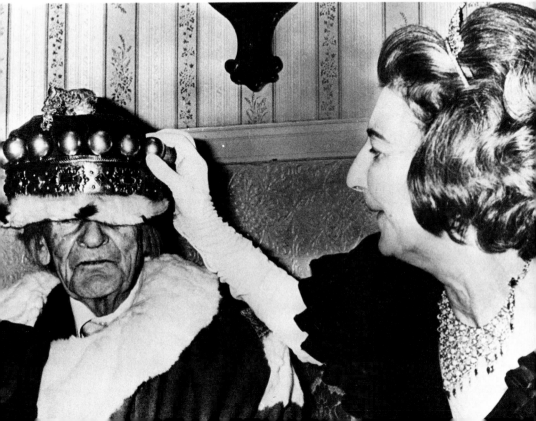

Kilkea Castle, Co. Kildare, which until 1960 was lived in by the
FitzGeralds.

Four generations: the seventh Duke of Leinster (right), the Marquess of
Kildare (left) with Viscount Leinster on his knee, and the Earl of Offaly
(centre). The portrait of the first Duke of Leinster by Reynolds is in the
background.

discuss this thing further, you already know where I stand in this matter so let it go. Anyway, don't you think that May Etheridge and yourself did plenty to drag the old name in the mud?

By the way, what became of her? The last I heard she had become a drug addict and attempted suicide. Too bad, she was physically a very beautiful woman, and if only her mind and morals had equalled her beauty of body she would have made a most charming duchess. Do you know Ted I feel deeply sorry for her as I verily beleive that brought up under different conditions and surrounded by different environments she would have made a fit wife for you. In fact I still maintain that you were partly to blame for what happened. You see Ted I am the same old Preacher and I still like to be fair and give even the devil his due.

Well, old Sap, this is a pretty long letter for me to write and I might change my mind and not send it you at all, but whatever happens I never shall have hard feelings towards you but for god's sake don't make me fight for my son's rights because if you do it will be a terrible battle.

As I told you, I kept my real identity from my wife and I don't beleive she has the least idea even today of what her children are entitled to, and now as things have gone this far I shall not tell her. She has done everything to get me back but I refuse to go now, and just recently she had me served with divorce papers and claims the sole rights of the children.

She thinks that rather than lose them I'd be willing to go back, but I am afraid she is too late and at present I am going to fight her for them. So that is the way things are at present, and I am awaiting her next move.

Well Ted there is very little else to write that would

interest you save that I am still on the look out for something new in the way of excitement. But recently I have
become acquainted with some very nice people and they
have treated me jolly decent considering my present
position and as far as they know I am just an ordinary
American bum. It surely does one good to have people
beleive in ones decency. If things were only different I
beleive I could get a new lease on life and too, perhaps gain
a little happiness; as it is I hate to trade further under false
colors.

But I surely am tempted to –

This curious, none too literate letter had evidently continued, but was torn off at this point. According to Vivien, it
had shaken the Marquess; it was the first intimation that his
succession might be challenged, and she wondered whether he
knew or suspected there was someone with a better claim to the
dukedom than himself, or even that he did not know precisely
what had happened to the sixth Duke.

The Marquess' reaction, as reported and interpreted by
Vivien, seemed incredible to Ford. The Marquess had always
been on good terms with the Mallaby-Deeleys; if he hadn't
heard the truth about the sixth Duke from his father he would
surely have heard it from the beneficiaries of his father's
inheritance. Ford wondered whether Vivien only believed in
Leonard's claim because she had seen the Marquess prosper
and her husband suffer through the arrangement with the
Mallaby-Deeleys. She had seen her stepson living in Kilkea or
Oxfordshire surrounded by family possessions while she and
her husband eked out an existence in bed-sitting-rooms. She
told Ford about the hard work she had undertaken to clear
Edward's long-standing bankruptcy, and how all her enquiries
into the Mallaby-Deeley agreement had been stalled.

Although Ford thought he had heard the whole of Vivien's story after their long meeting, they talked again on several subsequent occasions. Sometimes Vivien altered her original version; sometimes she vouchsafed new information. She now said the seventh Duke was secretive about other things than his elder brother; he used to get up very early in the morning to check the post, yet ten years before he died this habit had abruptly ceased, just about the time of Maurice Francis' death. Vivien said she knew nothing about Patricia's telegram, and pointed out that in 1967 they had been living in Malta, not in Sussex. When they went on their charity tour of America a few months before her husband's death, Vivien said he had been very nervy, quite unlike his usual self; perhaps the belated arrival of Maurice Francis' 'Dear Ted' letter had upset him, though he didn't admit it. Finally, to Ford's surprise, Vivien admitted that 'Fitz' had told her of another boy at Carton, whom he had heard but never seen.

One major drawback to Ford's investigation had been the dearth of contemporary witnesses; those he found still living in Ireland were very old, their memories unreliable. From Miss Grace Jackson, a neighbour mentioned by Maurice Francis, he was told that the rumour of there being four boys had long circulated in the district of Kilkea; from the wife of the gamekeeper, Arthur Inglis, he was informed that there was no room at Carton to hide a child, despite its sixty-four bedrooms. Inglis himself had played with the FitzGerald boys in the 1890s; he confirmed that the sixth Duke was subject to frequent fits, definitely before 1900. Inglis said he distinctly remembered the Duke lighting the bonfire at his coming of age celebrations in 1908, though according to the local paper the Duke was in London at the time. He added that Lord Frederick and Lady Nesta were very strict with the boys, and that

87

Edward was remembered for always getting into trouble, particularly with servant girls, sometimes causing them and their families to be sent away. Mrs Geraghty, keeper of the village shop in Maynooth and a daughter of one of the pall-bearers of 1922, told Ford the story of the dispute over the sixth Duke's coffin. Somewhere, she said, she had a photograph of the funeral, and would look it out for him; when Ford called on her again she announced that she had given it away to a friend.

Ford had little success with documentary research: the Kilkea Parish Baptismal Register only went back to 1906. The earlier records had disappeared, to the consternation of the vicar who had written in the new book: 'By order of His Grace the Lord Archbishop of Dublin I place on record the fact that in June 1905 the previous baptismal record was missing and I could not trace it though I made diligent search for it.' Also at Kilkea, Ford failed to find the tree houses in the grounds described by Maurice Francis which Patricia said she had found on her visit to Ireland. Curiously enough, numerous people remembered Patricia Roberts visiting the area in the early 1960s, when she herself maintained her first visit was in 1971. The eighth Duke later said that there could not have been any tree houses at Kilkea without his knowing about them; after all, he had lived there from 1949 to 1960.

But before Ford could conclude that his Irish visit had been fruitless, he made an important discovery. Under the tower of the church at Maynooth – the FitzGeralds' mausoleum before the consecration of the graveyard at Carton in 1887 – he found an unmarked child's coffin.

7

The Matrimonial Sensation

THE difficulties Ford had in discovering anything about the children were repeated in the case of their parents. Gerald, fifth Duke of Leinster, was one of fifteen children, four of whom died in their youth. Until he married – the papers announced his engagement as 'the matrimonial sensation of 1883' – he had the company of three bachelor brothers and three unmarried sisters. He preferred living quietly in Ireland to the London season; he spent a lot of time tidying and cataloguing the rare books in his huge library. Like his predecessors, the fifth Duke was not an absentee landlord, and the newspapers described him as popular with neighbours and tenants. The year he died he was remembered for having voted against the Home Rule Bill in the House of Lords.

When he and Hermione Duncombe married in January 1884 they lived first at Kilkea and at Hertford Street, London. Despite their prominence in Irish society, especially after Gerald succeeded the fourth Duke in 1887, they both preferred to give small parties and did not attend often at the Viceregal Court at Dublin Castle. The Viceroy, Lord Houghton, was not popular with the Irish gentry, but he was a cousin of Hermione's. When she was obliged to receive him at Carton once, she greeted him with the words, 'I receive you as cousin, not as

Viceroy,' and did not curtsey to him. Hermione, sometimes
rather silent at large gatherings, was capable of speaking very
bluntly at times. On another occasion Hermione whistled a
tune for the orchestra, and was rebuked for this 'unladylike
behaviour' by Lady Zetland, a relation by marriage to Lord
Elcho; a few days after this incident Lady Zetland made some
request of Hermione who responded with a flippant remark,
adding that Lady Zetland could jolly well do it herself. The
Zetlands made a great issue of this, to the obvious embarrassment and private displeasure of the Duke.

Apart from countless descriptions of her beauty there is little
written about Hermione, probably because of a married life led
in the seclusion of Carton and her early death. Clara Grant
Duff wrote, 'I have seen men in top hats running like hares
down Rotten Row to see the Duchess ride past on her big black
horse,' adding, 'but then in those days people cared less for
smartness and more for actual beauty.' Lord Ernest Hamilton
described the Duncombe daughters in glowing terms:

> All Lord Feversham's daughters were beautiful – aston-
> ishingly beautiful – but, if the four Yorkshire sisters had
> stood in competition before Paris, I think he would have
> given the apple to Lady Hermione . . . as a child of sixteen
> or so, when she and her sisters used to play about in
> Belgrave Square, her beauty was so dazzling as to be
> almost unbelievable. It was not only that she was divinely
> tall and absolutely flawless in shape, feature and complex-
> ion – a very rare combination – but she also had on her
> face that look of radiant goodness which, for some mys-
> terious reason, is seldom seen on the face of any except
> those doomed to an early death.

Hermione was the eldest of the four daughters – each of a
different father, it was said – born to the first Countess of

Feversham. The first Earl was of an old Yorkshire family ennobled in 1826. The eldest son died young, leaving an infant heir who himself died while serving in the King's Royal Rifles during the First World War. Another brother, Maurice Francis' 'favourite uncle Hubes', died without marrying according to all reference books, though this appears to have been far from the truth. Indeed, he seems to have had much in common with his nephew, the seventh Duke of Leinster. An article which appeared in an American newspaper in 1912 said that Hubert Duncombe

> ... spent some time in the United States in a kind of exile, for society here seems to have ignored his presence. While still a boy, having barely reached his majority, he had married a music hall artiste or variety actress, as she would be called in America. Old Lord Feversham, who is very proud of his lineage, was deeply offended and stopped the young man's allowance, which until then had been very liberal. Hubert Duncombe and his wife, who were neither of them of a saving disposition, ran heavily into debt, landing in the bankruptcy court. Then the old earl relented a little. He agreed to give his son an allowance of $2,000 a year on condition that he lived anywhere out of England. The pair came over here and drifted around from one city to another. Wearied of this life, they returned to England, when the lady went back to the stage and behaved in such a manner as to enable Hubert Duncombe to obtain a divorce.

Hubert's bravery in the South African War won him the DSO; he was an MP from 1895–1900. It appears he later married again, though neither marriage nor offspring are listed in *Burke's*. Patricia knew of his children through her father and it was from Hubert Duncombe's son that Leonard first heard of the seventh Duke taking his seat in the House of Lords.

Of Hermione's sisters, Helen was the nearest in age and most like her in looks; the two were very close in all things. Cynthia, the third daughter, was nominated co-guardian of Hermione's children after her death. Ulrica was very much the baby of the Duncombe family.

Maurice Francis and contemporary newspapers maintained that the Leinsters' marriage was supremely happy, and Ford was understandably surprised to find a whole chapter devoted to Hermione in a book by the Countess of Fingall which was distinctly at variance with the popular idea. 'Hermione's life was a sad one,' Lady Fingall said, 'and it must have seemed so beautiful to anyone looking in from outside.' Lady Fingall had not known Hermione when she lived at Kilkea and had composed the heartfelt if limping couplet:

> Kilkea Castle and Lord Kildare
> Are more than any woman can bear.

In 1887, when the fifth Duke and Duchess moved to Carton, Lady Fingall became a close friend of the family and frequently stayed in the house. She describes Hermione's astonishing beauty, and her talent for music, sculpture and gardening – the gardens she designed are still a feature of Carton. Hermione was highly artistic and found life with the Duke in the depths of the Irish countryside incompatible with her lively nature. 'The Duke was good and kind,' Lady Fingall wrote, 'but not the man for her. She wanted a man she could look up to and fear a little, as well as love.' She gathered this presumably from the long conversations they used to have late at night; Hermione used to creep into Lady Fingall's bedroom and curl up in front of the fire in her nightdress – 'that's how I know she had beautiful feet'. Lady Fingall described the entertaining at Carton as being small parties of Hermione's closest friends – Emily Lawless, the Dunravens, Bully Oliphant, Lord Elcho – with the occasional big reception; the Prince and Princess of Wales came once.

In following up these names and Hermione's relations, many of whom Patricia had heard about from her father, Ford made contact with the daughter of Ulrica Baring, Hermione's youngest sister, who had in her possession a bundle of letters which bore out Lady Fingall's description of Hermione's married life. The letters were written by Hermione to Helen, Viscountess d'Abernon, her favourite sister and confidante.

The picture of the Duke which appears in these letters is of an insensitive, tyrannical man, whom Hermione could neither please nor placate, though exactly what her efforts were in this direction is not clear. The lack of intimacy or friendship between the Duke and Duchess is described in Hermione's letter of 9 October 1890:

It is true things have been very blue ... no danger is imminent. I shall not go away, I am not dreaming of eloping. I shall not press Gerry to allow a judicial separation, and I'm not doing all I can to goad him into wishing it himself. On the contrary I have been trying to come within less immeasurable distance of his standards of excellence, so that if I cannot please him there may yet be less reasonable cause for complaint. But ... it is very difficult. We cannot understand each other and it is hopeless to expect we ever shall. If K. would only accept this fact (as I would willingly do), if we could agree to pull together, to keep up appearances before the world and live separate in our own lives and households – not trouble and weary each other by constant friction, there would yet be some possibility of things coming straight. But to this

93

Gerry will not agree. While admitting there is no love nor sympathy between us, he still insists upon trying to force me to become something different to what I am, or to what it lies in my nature to become. For this reason he uses petty tyranny on every imaginable sort of occasion.

Hermione had begun to study sculpture in 1890 and had mentioned to the Duke her desire to go to Paris to carry on her work in a year or so, but he did not approve of her new hobby.

If I had less vitality and less energy, I should not mind things so much, I should not be so rebellious, nor restless, nor so irritable. I have nothing on which to expend my energy, no object or aim in life, no great interest. If I was more domestic, I might have given all my mind to managing the house, but even here the field is not my own. It is not a housekeeper K. wants, it is an under-housekeeper. I may not choose my occupations – I thought this winter I would work hard at my modelling – but here is a fresh apple of discord. It is not an occupation K. approves of. Therefore I may not go upstairs to my painting room till (under his direction) I have performed my household duties, written my letters and *practised for one hour on the organ*, within his hearing. I may not have a fire there because the time I spend there is willful waste. I am humiliated before the servants; every order I give is counter-manded unless I have consulted K. about it first. And fault is found with me for anything and everything I do and say.

In the same undated letter Hermione goes on to the problems of having to share a bedroom with the Duke.

What I resent is that though K. has no more wish than I have that we should live *maritalement*, he still *insists* on

94

sleeping in my room *for fear of what the servants may think*! Even though he knows what a bad sleeper I am and that except alone! I cannot sleep. And that the servants have only to listen at the door to be aware that recrimination continues late into the night and begins early in the morning.

Yet in Lady Fingall's book she describes Hermione's 'small white room with a narrow bed like a girl's' which opened off her exquisitely furnished boudoir. She must have slept separately from the Duke at least some of the time, for he would not have allowed her to run around the house in her nightdress as Lady Fingall described. Whatever her feelings regarding living '*maritalement*' with the Duke, some eighteen months after this letter Hermione managed to produce Edward. She only once mentions the children in her correspondence with Helen, and there are no allusions to a permanent invalid or daughter; she refers to only two boys in a letter written the year before Edward was born. Hermione seems preoccupied with her own thoughts and feelings to the exclusion of all else. In April 1891 she bemoans the wet Irish spring 'and the prospect of the years and years before me in which I see nothing but solitude, dreariness and fossilization'. Somewhat incoherently she also refers to a recent escapade – or discovery – for which she knows the Duke would rebuke her severely.

I am *irresponsible*. Do not think anyone has told me this – I hope perhaps nobody has guessed it? but now that I have found it out, that I *know* it, it explains everything that I could not understand, even myself, before – I have tried to deceive even myself about before, and until I feel that I am sober enough and calm enough to have *complete* control over myself, I will go out *no more*. If Kildare could understand, I would tell him everything, and ask him to help me. But if he knew all he would only think me hopelessly wicked and vicious and I am *not*, I am *not that*! My better self has perhaps left me for a little, but it will come back to me, I know it will. I am horrified and disgusted at the shallowness of my present ways and feelings, but there used to be deep pools somewhere and I will find them again. You don't know what I have been through lately, the humiliation, the despondency, and the despair and the *loneliness* – who will, who could understand such a hopeless and complex frame of mind!

Hermione concluded enigmatically with, 'One helping hand has been unexpectedly stretched out to me, and in your absence, till your return, to that hand I will cling.' Who the hand belonged to Ford could not discover – Hermione evidently felt mistrustful of naming names in her letters. Over the following two years the problems of life at Carton were passed on to Helen in similarly despairing terms. In August 1893 Helen wrote to the Duke on her sister's behalf, suggesting

... more freedom should be secured to her and in which it should be agreed that seven or eight months per annum is the limit of time she should be expected to pass at Carton. No one can regret more than I do that such a compact should have become necessary, but the circumstances of your married life have been peculiar to the highest degree and I think that after consideration you will not fail to recognize that in common fairness and equity she has a right to some of the liberty on her side that you exercise so freely on your own ... I only write in order to express a hope that you may see your way to some agreement independently of all publicity and without other arbitration than that of justice and commonsense.

The Duke replied by telegram: 'Thank you for your letter and advice. Hope to act on it.'

But there was little time to do so. After the Leinsters returned from staying with the Duke of Argyll at Inverary, the Duke caught typhoid fever and died. Although he had been ill for a fortnight he was not thought to be in any danger, and his death came as a great shock. He was buried at Carton very quietly; only the immediate family attended his funeral. Even Lady Fingall, who said she got on very well with the Duke, did not drive over for the service.

Before he died the Duke may have taken his sister-in-law's advice in respect of his daily treatment of his wife, for Hermione wrote soon afterwards:

> Those last weeks we spent together in Scotland he was very dear and kind to me – kinder and dearer perhaps than he had ever been – and my last recollections of him are of tenderness and love ... And now he is dead, I remember only his merits, his dearness to me in many ways, the strong foundation of love and affection that underlay his apparent coldness. He did everything, managed every-thing – took the whole burden of life from my shoulders – and now I am conscious of a great blank. A feeling that the arms of a silent encircling love have been withdrawn. No words can express his goodness and patience all through his illness ... these last few days have been a terrible strain and the misery of each hopeless detail haunts me day and night.

There must indeed have been a complete change in the Duke and Duchess' regard for each other; it is touchingly expressed in a poem Hermione wrote soon after her husband's death in December 1893.

Kind words unspoken
Must silent remain;
A hard heart broken
To the dead is no gain.

Cruel lips, cold as stone,
Accustomed to hate,
Have sometimes to own
Sweet words came too late.

Words may come sighing,
Hard hearts may relent,
What use to the dying
Whose days here are spent?

Some say 'God wills it',
And some say – ''Tis Fate',
My heart – and none stills it –
Says, You loved him too late.

Ford regretted that he could not find any letters written by the Duke. The picture of domestic repression Hermione had given her sister was a subjective one, yet Helen's phrase 'the circumstances of your married life have been peculiar to the highest degree' indicated that Hermione's reactions to life at Carton were not entirely the hysterical ravings of a gifted and petulant girl unwilling to be shackled to a stubborn Irish nobleman and his austere mansion.

Whatever the truth, Hermione threw herself into sculpting and painting as soon as she was made a widow. Naturally, Lady Fingall had not commented significantly on the Leinsters' family life, but she described Hermione's movements for the last eighteen months of her life with less circumspection.

Hermione spent a lot of time with two friends in a cottage outside London, studying painting. Although G. F. Watts had begun a portrait of Hermione, the curator of the Watts Gallery said that there was no record of the Duchess of Leinster being a pupil of his, as Maurice Francis had described. Already Hermione's fatal illness was beginning to show itself; Lady Fingall vividly remembered an occasion when Hermione appeared unannounced at her house in London.

> She was still wearing black ... and nothing ever became her beauty better. She had bright colour in her cheeks and she was panting as if she had run up the stairs, being in such a hurry with the news she had to tell me. I never saw her colour more brilliant but she was very thin ... 'I must tell you,' she said, excited as a girl who had received a proposal. 'You won't believe it! The doctors have just told me I have only a year to live, and even to live that year I must go abroad at once. ...' She was to cross that night to Dublin to speak to the girls at the Alexandria School where she had founded the Hermione Lectures. 'Only a year to live,' she repeated, and that wonderful smile of hers lit my wintry room as though spring had suddenly come into it, 'I think I must tell the girls. Wouldn't they think it a joke?'

But, as Lady Fingall added, it was no joke, for she did not even live a year. On 20 March 1895 she died at the Hôtel des Iles Britanniques at Mentone – coincidentally where the Prince of Wales was staying. She was only thirty years old. It is said that she died in the arms of Lord Elcho, with whom she had had a liaison lasting some years. To Lady Fingall reticence was the better part of friendship; discretion prevented her from admitting some of the 'many things' Hermione had told her 'that I may not speak of' although she added, 'Hermione said

99

to me once that all the people she loved had been taken away from her.'

The Duchess of Leinster's body was brought back to Carton where she was buried at her husband's side. She had written her own epitaph: 'My God, I know that all thou ordainest is for the best, and I am content.' At her funeral, which was far better attended than her husband's, wreaths arrived from the Prince of Wales and friends and relations all over England and Ireland.

After the fifth Duke's death Lord Frederick and Lady Nesta had looked after Carton while Lord Walter and the other aunts lived at Kilkea. Now Hermione was dead Lord Frederick and Lady Cynthia Graham took over the legal responsibility of bringing up the young Duke and his brothers. By this time their uncle Charles had emigrated to Australia, as Maurice Francis told his family, for reasons which were not clear, and George spent most of his life abroad on diplomatic service. The fifth Duke's other brother, Maurice, died in 1901 leaving a widow, Adelaide, who later became the guardian of the seventh Duke's son Gerald when the child was taken away from May. Patricia presumed this was the aunt her father referred to when he spoke of his aunt Ada, though she was always called 'aunt Adie' in the family. Henry, the uncle whom Maurice Francis described as having something to do with public records, was at one time involved in *army* records, but by 1930 – when Maurice Francis said this uncle gave him new papers to return to America – he had in fact retired.

In the sixth Duke's minority Frederick administered the seventy thousand acres of the Leinster Estates, with the help of the family lawyer. It was during this time that Maurice Francis claimed his uncles had apportioned or sold off the estates for their own benefit. Much of the blame for this was laid on George Wyndham, an MP and descendant of the second Duke of Leinster. Maurice Francis also mentioned the Earl of Dun-raven and Edgar Vincent, who had taught him his superb horsemanship. While it was true that Wyndham was involved in the sale of Leinster land after the 1903 Land Act it was as a proponent of the parliamentary act bearing his name, not as an individual, or on behalf of the FitzGerald family. Lord Dun-raven had in the 1890s provided much of the initiative for a land act, and he had also spent some time in Wyoming, the state where Patricia first traced movements of her father. Edgar Vincent, Viscount d'Abernon, was certainly a close friend of Hermione's; it was on one of his frequent visits to Carton that he and Hermione's sister Helen announced their engagement.

One American newspaper suggested that the sale of Fitz-Gerald property had all but bankrupted the provisions of the 1903 Act, but this was totally inaccurate; other newspapers mentioned over one million, or two million pounds. No one knows exactly how much the trustees of the Leinster Estates received. Although some of the money may have found its way to Frederick and Walter the small amounts they left in their wills make this unlikely.

Despite the interest and involvement of so many FitzGerald relations in the care and administration of the Leinster Estates, the irresponsible Edward was able only ten years later to mortgage his birthright to Mallaby-Deeley. It was as though this action heralded the end of the FitzGeralds' position in Ireland; within another ten years most of Edward's close FitzGerald relations were dead.

8

Off the Record

ARLY in January 1977 James Arthur finally obtained permission to examine the asylum's file on the Duke of Leinster. Patricia was anxious to have confirmation of certain medical details of the inmate, whom she imagined must have been Frederick, the fourth child. If she believed her father's story she had to assume that someone else died in 1922. Claiming a familial relationship with the inmate, she asked the authorities to permit Dr Arthur to see the records which were now kept in the Records Registry in Edinburgh. He would then be able to report back to Patricia.

After spending an hour and a half studying the record, James Arthur was convinced that, notwithstanding all external evidence to the contrary, the inmate and the sixth Duke of Leinster had not been the same man. He also thought that the file had been edited, not after the event, but at the time of its compilation. This seemed to him to be the only possible explanation for its astonishing brevity. No attempt was made to conceal the condition of madness in the inmate. There was no note of genital abnormality, but James Arthur thought certain statements made by the inmate, which he was not permitted to reveal, buttressed the 'girl' theory.

The slimness of a file purporting to be a record of thirteen years' insanity might, James Arthur reasoned, be explained by the inmate's living in a private bungalow where he could receive visitors without their names being recorded. There was evidence that during periods of good health he had been allowed out in the company of a keeper. He had played golf at least once, and he had been allowed to send a telegram from the local post office. This struck James Arthur as very odd: if he could send his own telegrams why had his letter to Mr Clyde been intercepted and kept in the file? Why should the authorities try to prevent the inmate's identity being known in the outside world when he was in a position to make it known himself? Perhaps the letter had been planted in order to convey the impression that it was the Duke who was incarcerated for, contrary to what McGuire had been told on the telephone, there *was* a photograph of the inmate in the file. It was the same as the one which featured in the *Winnipeg Free Press Prairie Farmer* in August 1922. When James Arthur referred back to Patricia, she said the photograph had been taken in Dublin some time before June 1909. However, the thought of any other investigator having access to the Craighouse file perturbed her and, after receiving James Arthur's report, she wrote to the authorities asking them to seal it.

Ford asked Arthur whether there was anything in the file which could verify the signatures on the last three codicils to the sixth Duke's will. Nothing appeared in the Craighouse file for the three dates on which the Duke had signed them. This, Arthur thought, confirmed that the file had been edited or was drastically incomplete, or even that it had not been the inmate who had signed the codicils. In the third codicil, dated 1 February 1912, the Duke requested that his portrait by the Scottish painter Fiddes Watt be placed on his death with the other portraits entailed with the dukedom . When Ford tried to find the portrait, neither the eighth Duke nor any other member of the FitzGerald family had it; it had not been sold in the seventh Duke's bankruptcy auction in 1926; the Scottish, Irish and English National Galleries had never heard of it; it was not mentioned in the artist's relevant diaries.

The signatures on the will and codicils matched the writing in the letter to Mr Clyde, and were similar to the handwriting in the debating book at Eton. Sir Fergus Graham, the Duke's cousin, also identified signatures in the Netherby Hall visitors' book, dated 1905 and 1906, as those of the Duke, and they too matched those on the will and codicils.

Sir Fergus had further evidence regarding the sixth Duke of Leinster which only came out at the time of Leonard's claim in 1976. A year before this the seventh Duke, applying for his Writ of Summons, had been obliged to produce evidence corroborating his identity, as all peers have to do, and Sir Fergus Graham had been asked to swear an affidavit to the effect that the seventh Duke was the fifth Duke's son, which he did. But when Leonard made his claim Sir Fergus had sworn a further document, categorically denying any truth in Maurice Francis' stories. He swore that four children had been born to the fifth Duke, one of whom, a girl, had died in infancy; he had been brought up with the three boys. His mother, Lady Cynthia Graham, had been asked by her sister to undertake the upbringing of the three boys, and they had often come to Netherby. Sir Fergus had also been with his cousins to Duncombe Park, but he had hardly ever been to Carton – his cousins spent very little time there. In this second document Sir Fergus affirmed that the photograph of the fair-haired Duke published at the time of the Coronation in 1902 was indeed of Leinster. Sir Fergus then went on:

Leinster had always suffered from ill-health and it was known in the family that he also suffered from epilepsy.

Consequently he needed a considerable amount of care and attention and after he left Eton he had to have a 'tutor' to look after him. Some time after leaving Eton, not very long, the family found Dr Pollock of Edinburgh, who was then a promising young doctor, to look after Leinster and he went to live with him in London first and then they moved to Edinburgh. After this I did not see much of Leinster; I do not recollect his coming to Netherby after I left Eton in 1910. But I did see him once or twice in Edinburgh at Dr Pollock's house and several times when he was in London with Dr Pollock ... I cannot be precise when I saw Leinster in Edinburgh. When Leinster died in February 1922 I was bidden by my father to join Dr Pollock at Carlisle; he came from Edinburgh. The coffin accompanied us on the trip. We went to Carton and we attended the funeral. A few years ago, I cannot be precise, I received a letter which I have not kept from a Mrs Roberts from America claiming to be some descendant of 'Maurice'. I paid no attention to it as it seemed complete rubbish to me. I had and have never heard in the family or anywhere any suggestion that Leinster, who died on 2 February 1922, was not the sixth Duke of Leinster. I knew him, I was brought up with him and if it is suggested that my mother was a party to some dishonesty then I can only say that such an idea is unthinkable. The same applies to Dr Pollock (later Sir Donald Pollock) and Leinster's uncle Lord Frederick FitzGerald who signed the death certificate; though I never knew Lord Frederick well he was much respected in the family. Equally a great many other people must have been involved and I must have known if anything out of the ordinary had taken place. To suggest that Leinster, the sixth Duke, could have been accepted by any branch of the armed forces of England, the United States or Canada is quite unthinkable. He could never have passed any medical examination. He needed constant care and attention at all times.

The document certainly had a formidable tone, although Sir Fergus' affirmations were largely based on family hearsay; he himself was too young to have had first-hand knowledge of the oldest child, and he only saw the sixth Duke a few times after he was grown up. Ford was intrigued that he made no mention of Craighouse, or of the Duke being mad, but the evidence, especially that of the handwriting, seemed to suggest that the inmate of Craighouse *was* the Duke of Leinster.

There remained the question of epilepsy. Sir Fergus stated that it was known in the family that the Duke suffered from it, but when had this first been discovered? The twenty-five years recorded on the death certificate would have meant the Duke suffered from it three years before going to Eton, five years before the Coronation. Another cousin, Brigadier Denis Fitz-Gerald, too young to have met the Duke, maintained that it was only after he left Eton that his epilepsy became apparent. Brigadier FitzGerald had not been told directly about it, but had overheard his parents discussing an incident: his mother, wife of the fifth Duke's youngest brother, Lord Henry Fitz-Gerald, had been shopping in Sloane Street with the young Duke soon after he had left school. Suddenly the Duke fell to the pavement. Lady Henry, not knowing what was happening, hurried into a chemist's shop. On seeing the Duke the chemist evidently showed surprise that Lady Henry didn't know the Duke was having a fit.

But if epilepsy was the Duke's only complaint, why had his absences from Eton been so regular? The newspapers had stated that the Duke suffered from a weak chest – and there could be no reason for the FitzGeralds to conceal this – but no mention of it appears in the Craighouse file prior to the Duke's fatal bout of lobar pneumonia.

The one piece of evidence casting the gravest doubts on the identity of the 'prisoner' at Craighouse was not, in the end, of a medical nature. It was a letter from Lady Cynthia Graham to Dr Pollock which Arthur had found in the Duke's Craighouse file. In it Lady Cynthia, apparently fearful of the inmate escaping, insisted that on absolutely no account should he be given her address. If the inmate was Maurice, sixth Duke of Leinster, he surely knew exactly where she lived. Had not her son, Sir Fergus, stated that the Duke was practically brought up at Netherby Hall?

9

A Man of Many Names

PATRICIA's father had never attempted to conceal his use of pseudonyms within his family circle. Indeed, his borrowed names were as much a family joke as were his different birthdays. When he was first in Wyoming he used the name Charlie Tyler; several friends still remembered him by this name. At other times, Patricia maintained, he called himself A. B. Anderson; when writing short stories, poems and articles he used the *noms de plume* Monte FitzGerald and Bennet Foster.

Patricia had an explanation for the name Charlie Tyler, and the rest of the family were in accord with it. Their father had been very good friends at school with a boy or boys from South Wales named Tyler. When Maurice Francis had arrived in America, he had been anxious to keep out of touch with his family and had taken the name Tyler and used it until June 1916 when, as Francis FitzGerald, he had joined the Canadian Overseas Expeditionary Force. The Tyler at school must have been a very good friend; Maurice Francis had christened Patricia 'Patricia Tyler FitzGerald' and when she asked him why he said it was 'in order to identify you'. But Patricia's efforts to learn anything from the Tylers of Glamorgan had resulted in nothing.

As to A. B. Anderson, the explanations were rather more bizarre. Maurice Francis' forwarding address on leaving the Canadian Army in November 1918 was 'A. B. Anderson, 114 Spence Street, Winnipeg'; among his papers there was a postcard addressed to Anderson at that address. Apparently his family was using detectives to track him down, and Maurice Francis 'coming across a body somewhere' had exchanged papers; when the body was found by the authorities it had been dispatched to Ireland where it caused his family some distress. Nobody knew where this extraordinary incident had taken place, or what had been Maurice Francis' exact relationship with the unfortunate Anderson. In any case, no one had anything but vague memories to rely on; there was no evidence of Maurice Francis using the name, and none of his surviving friends knew him by it. At the same time no one expressed surprise that he might have taken another name, or that his coming across a body (in the Wild West) was anything out of the ordinary. One possible explanation, although very prosaic, occurred to Ford: anyone called Anderson would invariably be placed at the head of any list and this could be useful to someone anxious to avoid bureaucratic delays. Ford turned up one possible candidate for the body which Maurice Francis had supposedly found. One of the victims after the *Empress of Ireland* sank in the St Lawrence River in 1913 was named A. B. Anderson. There was also a first lieutenant of that name serving in the Canadian Army in England during the First World War whose court martial for stealing petrol was widely publicized.

Since the beginning of the enquiry, Ford had been perplexed by the use of the name Francis, since he had seen no mention of it in anything concerning the sixth Duke. This was understandable, for on obtaining the sixth Duke's birth certificate he had seen that Maurice FitzGerald, Marquess of Kildare, had no middle name. Lord Desmond, Lord Edward and the fifth

Duke also had no middle name. The FitzGeralds were not remarkable in this practice, commonly found in noble families at the time, of giving their children one Christian name only. Needless to say, as on so many other confusing details, Patricia was able to enlighten Ford on her father's use of the name Francis, and offered the ready explanation that Maurice Francis was not his real name!

This time her revelations concerned her father's deportation from America in 1930 (apparently through the machinations of his father-in-law, David Gough) for having faulty papers. At the time Patricia's father was involved in a lengthy divorce case, and his father-in-law, influential in the Arizona State Legislature, wanted him completely out of the way. But David Gough's action was not as successful as he had hoped. Maurice Francis went to Canada, and said he had only to write to Lord Henry FitzGerald, his uncle, to receive 'proper papers'. Almost immediately, under the name of Maurice Francis FitzGerald, he was allowed to return.

However, Ford found another reason which might have caused Maurice Francis' deportation. In 1929 the American Government revised its immigration laws: whereas an Englishman had needed only a letter of credit or reference to live in the country, he now had to produce further proof of identity. Maurice Francis had somehow been sent the identity papers of a man whose name closely approximated to that of the late Duke of Leinster, the implication being that the 'real Duke' was no longer prepared to masquerade under a false name. But this was hardly convincing for Patricia's father had been using the name Francis since 1916.

Moreover, on the occasion of his first marriage (12 April 1919), when he was calling himself Francis Maurice Fitz-Gerald, he had given names for his parents which had no connection to the fifth Duke and Duchess of Leinster. Instead he named his parents as Frederick Charles FitzGerald and Emma Webb. On his Canadian Army Attestation Certificate the name of his next-of-kin was someone else still, a Mrs C. Knock, c/o the King's Royal Rifle Corps Barracks, Winchester. Maurice Francis had mentioned that his father and uncles were members of the King's Royal Rifles. Certainly Lord Walter and Lord Frederick FitzGerald had been but, according to their records, the fifth Duke of Leinster had at no time served in the regiment.

When Patricia's father married for the second time he gave no parental names or his date of birth, but when he married for the third time in 1965, using the name Maurice Francis Fitz-Gerald, he gave his date of birth as 10 June 1888, its place as Dublin, and his parents' names as Patrick FitzGerald and Mary Kennedy.

Patricia thought this last identity was false. She said it was testimony to her father's bona fides that he did nothing to conceal his chameleon identity, and testimony to her honesty that she passed on all documents, whether deleterious to her father's story or not. To Ford, it was significant that Patricia's father had taken the names of real persons, which is vital if you have to provide papers. For some reason, though, Maurice Francis had always taken pains to emphasize some kind of personal connection with the actual bearers of the names he assumed.

Patricia's father could not in fact have known the real Maurice Francis FitzGerald, son of Patrick FitzGerald and Mary Kennedy, though the House of Lords, when investigating Leonard's claim, had been satisfied that this was his identity. They had acquired a certified copy dated 22 July 1930 of the birth certificate from the General Register Office, Dublin. But the House of Lords did not bother to look for a death certificate for this person. Ford did, and learned that the real

Maurice Francis FitzGerald had died in Dublin in 1888 when he was six weeks old.

There was now only one date of birth to be accounted for: 24 January 1887. This was the date given by Patricia's father when, as Francis FitzGerald, he had joined the Canadian Army in 1916, and the earliest of the three dates which had caused such mirth among his family when they celebrated his last 'real' birthday on 1 March 1967.

Ford was ready to agree that these name changes could have been expected from a man seeking anonymity. But if Patricia's father could assume new names or readopt old ones so easily, why should he not have gone one step further and assumed a whole identity, modifying his past as the mood took him? And why should his daughter, desperate to sustain belief in her father, not change it in her turn?

The story had changed in one crucial respect after Maurice Francis' death. Dermot Morrah's brief of 1969 stated: 'The contention of the dossier is that Maurice Francis and the sixth Duke of Leinster were the same person.' There was no reference to his having been 'rightful Duke after 1922'. In a letter to Charles Graves, Morrah had suggested that if the story had been concocted by conscious deception 'it can only be by Mrs Roberts herself'. Here Ford felt Morrah was mistaken, for as far as he could see, if anyone had been deceived, that person was Patricia. She had a reasonable explanation for the change in the story: she only transcribed her father's tapes some time after her correspondence with Morrah. But the errors of fact concerning the courtesy title, the FitzGerald family, Edward VII's Coronation and the division of the Leinster Estates in Ireland all undermined the credibility of the story, and the arrangement between Lord Edward and Mallaby-Deeley its logic.

Even so, Patricia remained convinced. The quest for her father's recognition had become nothing less than a vocation; she had also made new friends, acquired a surrogate family and a vast network of putative relations. On his part, Leonard simply wished to know who his father was. Patricia had none of Leonard's nagging uncertainties, for she had only happy memories of her childhood. It was unfortunate that other people were suspicious, but then they had not known her father as she had. She welcomed strangers who showed an interest in the case, bombarding them with effusive letters, diligent transcripts of tape-recordings, endless lists of names and addresses, newspaper cuttings and photographs. It was clear that, whatever she might say to the contrary, she was as much caught up in the mystery as anyone.

The story was undoubtedly far-fetched. With wicked uncles, a young man reared to play the part of a duke, an escape engineered by collaborating aunts, kidnap attempts and detectives, the Wild West, a secret and illegal 'abdication' agreement, a family secret too terrible to reveal – it was all fabulously melodramatic. Nevertheless, Maurice Francis' reticence on his past and his air of verisimilitude and genuine injury whenever he did speak of it, coupled with a knowledge of details that could, it was thought, only have been possessed by an intimate of the FitzGeralds, had combined to attract even the most sceptical towards acceptance of a tale whose credibility lay in its unlikelihood. The wild behaviour of the seventh Duke, and the ignorance and confusion occluding the life of the sixth Duke, contributed to its plausibility. And yet the old man *had* lied, even to his own family.

Ford wondered whether he could believe anything Maurice Francis had said, and if he should continue his research. He was no longer receiving any remuneration from Patricia but he still informed her when he found something. It gave him no pleasure to undermine her most cherished beliefs. It was nine months since he had received the telex that started his investigations; by May 1977 the only answers he could find were themselves questions. When he had begun he had been aware that Leonard's whole case could be resolved by a photograph of the sixth Duke, and it was strange that in the eight years between the death of Maurice Francis and the announcement of Leonard's claim no one had managed to find one. Now Ford had not one but four photographs of the sixth Duke of Leinster. Though they little resembled each other they did not look like Maurice Francis. Ford was sure that Patricia's father was not the Duke, nor even Maurice Francis FitzGerald – but he still had no idea of the man's real identity. There was no sign of the evidence that Maurice Francis had repeatedly said was 'all there'.

In March 1977, Tom McGuire came to England. Even if he was never going to find answers to all his questions, he was determined to fulfil Leonard's basic quest, to find a father with a true identity. McGuire's arrival gave Ford new enthusiasm. Together they might be able to prove at least part of Maurice Francis' story; perhaps he was an illegitimate son of the fifth Duke or one of his brothers. Maurice Francis had lied, but he had nonetheless a first-hand knowledge of the FitzGeralds.

McGuire felt sure that Maurice Francis had wanted his children to find his real identity and that somewhere among his effects there must exist a deliberate clue. Ford, on the other hand, thought that Maurice Francis, by his eightieth year, had come to believe his own many stories, however conflicting, and completely lost sight of his real past. Maurice Francis' pose as an ex-duke had proved successful, although without financial benefit, in that he had provoked much interest when he was alive, obituaries as far afield as San Francisco and Sydney,

Australia when he died, and set his son off on what he must have known could only be a forlorn and embarrassing quest. By informing only a small circle of his 'real' identity he had forestalled any public challenge.

McGuire had had a good look at the things Patricia's father had left: a suitcase filled with sheet music and mainly unintelligible manuscripts, a collection of old photographs, mostly of cowboys, a blotter on which could be discerned the words 'General Post Office, Edinburgh' and a few apparently meaningless papers, envelopes, postcards and letters. There was a Christmas card from 'Floss and Sid', an envelope from North Berwick. There was a simple silk scarf, 'a gift from Princess Mary', and an inscribed cigarette case, which Patricia said was a 'memento from an Indian prince'. There were military decorations, Coronation coins, medallions struck to commemorate royal visits to the Dominions; among several pieces of jewellery there was a starburst of diamonds and pearls mentioned, Patricia said, in the *Yorkshire Gazette*'s list of Hermione's wedding-presents. There was an Amati violin and a woman's gold watch inscribed 30 March 1864, the day of Hermione's birth. There was a bundle of photographs of the military funeral of one Lance-Corporal Tyler.

McGuire wondered if these photographs might be a clue to Maurice Francis' identity. He had after all given Patricia the name Tyler 'in order to identify her' and told her to go to the Tylers if she wanted to know the truth. Perhaps Patricia had contacted the wrong family of Tylers. McGuire had noted the name of the photographer, Lawrence of Gosport, on the back of one of the prints and determined to follow this lead up when he arrived in England.

McGuire and Ford found Lawrence of Gosport's telephone number, but were told that most of their records and negatives had been destroyed during the war. They suggested checking with the Naval Hospital in charge of Portsmouth Cemetery. The only Tyler buried there did not connect with the Tyler under investigation, and McGuire and Ford were referred to Gosport Town Hall. In the small military graveyard at Gosport they found the grave of Lance-Corporal Edwin Amand Tyler, a bandsman in the first battalion, the King's Royal Rifles, who was laid to rest on 2 August 1911.

Ford obtained his birth and death certificates from Somerset House. Edwin Tyler had died aged only twenty-three on 31 July 1911 at the New Barracks, Gosport, of a gunshot wound. The cause of death was 'wilful murder'.

When Ford spoke to the Regimental Record-Keeper he was nonplussed, for he had no record whatsoever of this incident. He told Ford he would be grateful for any information. Ford set about finding it, though he was baffled that the regiment had no documents relating to the murder as it had received widespread publicity in the local and national press. According to the defence, Richard Edge had been cleaning his rifle in the barracks when it had suddenly gone off. The shot hit and killed Tyler, lying on a nearby bed. At the time of the arrest, however, Edge's gun-cleaning materials were found neatly stowed in a box at the end of his bed. He could not explain why his rifle had been loaded at the time. No cartridges were allowed in barracks. No one heard Edge charge the rifle, and it was suggested that he had forgotten to empty his rifle after shooting practice.

At the trial, despite seemingly overwhelming evidence for the prosecution, it was decided that Edge did not have 'the makings of a killer' and that he was not the sort to bear ill-will towards a comrade who had his duty to do. The day before his death, Tyler had reported Edge for failing to answer roll-call; Edge claimed he had been too drunk to answer. Although he said at the trial that he and Tyler had been good chums for years, this had not prevented him from threatening to shoot his chum – flippantly, it was described by others – for reporting him.

In the end he was found not guilty, the reason being that no one had actually seen him load or level the murder weapon. Tyler, because of the circumstances of his death, was buried with full military honours.

A connection between Edwin Tyler and Maurice Francis FitzGerald was to be found in Tyler's birth certificate. He was born on the Isle of Wight on 19 February 1888, the son of Frederick Tyler and Emma Webb. On his first marriage certificate, Maurice Francis had given the names of his parents as Frederick Charles FitzGerald and Emma Webb.

But before McGuire and Ford could find more on the Tylers, they left for Scotland to meet James Arthur. They listened to endless tales of aristocratic intrigue and duplicity, and fruitlessly went over the ground they had each covered. They failed to gain permission to see the Craighouse file, which Patricia had caused to be sealed after the contents had been revealed to her, but they did manage, at last, to see Sir Fergus Graham. At a previous attempt Sir Fergus had been cool and dismissive; this time, he said, they were welcome to drop in at Netherby Hall.

To Ford's surprise, and contrary to what he had been led to expect by the gruff tone of the affidavit, Sir Fergus and Lady Graham were greatly intrigued by everything Ford told them. When he was shown a number of photographs, Sir Fergus had been unable to recognize one of Patricia's father but had picked out the Winnipeg photograph as representing the man he had known as Leinster. He had never used the Duke's Christian name; he was always 'Kildare' or 'Leinster'. He added that it must be remembered that the sixth Duke was eight years his senior and that they had not mixed much or communicated. Sir Fergus had been a great friend of the seventh Duke, whom he knew as 'Eddie'. Leinster had known Netherby well, and was very knowledgeable about the Navy, particularly submarines; Dr Pollock had entered as his recreation in *Who's Who* 'teaching young lads about ships'.

Sir Fergus went on to mention Robert, chauffeur to the Graham family, who had died recently. He had driven the boys to and from Eton and had known the FitzGerald boys very well. Of the Duke he used to say, 'Leinster was never the same after he left Eton.' During this period Sir Fergus had encountered the Duke several times at Pollock's London house. He had not attended the coming of age celebrations at Carton or Kilkea. Neither he nor his wife could offer an explanation for the disappearance of the fourth Duke's will or the Kilkea parish records.

Lady Graham considered it possible that Maurice Francis might be an illegitimate FitzGerald, or son of Hermione, to whom, she added, the fifth Duke had behaved appallingly. Both she and her husband were baffled by the dearth of photographs of and interviews with the sixth Duke. They did not say it outright, but it was apparent to Ford throughout their discussion that the Grahams thought Maurice Francis might well be related to the Duke; they never dismissed the claim out of hand. Although Sir Fergus mentioned that Leinster's epilepsy was known, he added that he had never seen the Duke have a fit; he said his mother had always believed Leinster to have a weak heart, and remembered that she had been given a hymnal by Leinster inscribed 'Aunt Cyn. Xmas 1910, Leinster'. Maurice Francis had said he had done this. Overall, Sir Fergus concluded, Leinster had always appeared perfectly normal.

There was confusion on one count: Sir Fergus insisted that the photograph of the plump boy holding a straw hat published at the time of the Duke's visit to the House of Commons in 1901 bore no resemblance whatsoever to any member of the family. Whether another meeting would have clarified the question of the photographs of the Duke, Ford never had a chance to find out, for a few months later Sir Fergus Graham died.

10

The Bandmaster

ON his return from Netherby, Ford began to investigate the background of the unfortunate Edwin Tyler. The records of the King's Royal Rifles – the one source that might have provided personal details – vouchsafed nothing. He had already sent the National Army Museum a number of unidentified photographs of men in uniform found among Maurice Francis' papers in the hope that they might at least be able to identify the regiments but, so far, he had heard nothing.

From Edwin Tyler's birth certificate Ford had his parents names, and from this their marriage certificate. On 10 January 1883, at the Registry Office, Pembroke, South Wales, Emma Webb had married Frederick John Tyler, a sergeant in the second battalion, the Royal Welch Fusiliers, stationed at Pembroke Dock. He was twenty-five, his father's name given as George Tyler, veterinary surgeon; she was twenty-one, the daughter of Sidney Webb, photographer. By the time of Edwin's birth in 1888 Frederick Tyler had changed regiments and been appreciably promoted; he was then the Bandmaster of the first battalion, the King's Royal Rifles.

Tracing other children of the marriage was not easy. Ford decided to start with the Isle of Wight, and found that there on

24 January 1887, at the Barracks, Parkhurst, Emma Webb had given birth to another son. His birth certificate was registered on 2 March 1887 – one day after the birth of Maurice, Marquess of Kildare. This date of birth was the third claimed by Maurice Francis to be accounted for. The son was christened Charles Alexander Tyler.

Ford could find no record of a marriage in England for either Edwin or Charles, nor could he find a death certificate for the latter. He found their father's death certificate, and from that he managed to find a will. Under the name Frederick Amand Tyler he had died on 20 May 1926, leaving an estate valued at £97. The residue was bequeathed to his widow, Rose Mary Tyler, and there were bequests to two sons – Frederick Tyler, Company Sergeant Major in the first battalion, the King's Royal Rifles, and Sidney Tyler, Company Quartermaster Sergeant, of the same battalion. There was no mention of Charles Alexander.

Sidney Tyler died in 1952. In his will he left a bequest to a son, Patrick, whom Ford was able to locate through the telephone directory. Patrick Tyler knew nothing about his family, except that his mother's name had been Florence. This offered a plausible explanation for the Christmas card found among Maurice Francis' papers from 'Floss and Sid'.

Ford still felt that there might be more than a mere regimental connection between the Tylers and the FitzGeralds, so he tried the Irish records. He found that the eldest son, Frederick Sidney, was born at the Barracks, Limerick, on 26 January 1885; Sidney was born in December of the same year at the Barracks, Kinsale, County Cork. Ford also traced their mother's death certificate: Emma Tyler, *née* Webb, had died at Pembroke Dock on 2 April 1915, the causes given as 'puerperal mania (chronic) 27 years and exhaustion'. Puerperal mania is a nervous condition resulting from childbearing; if twenty-seven years was the correct figure, the mania must have commenced with the birth of the youngest of the four boys, Edwin.

Following up the name Rose Mary Tyler, mentioned as widow in the Bandmaster's will, Ford found a record of his second marriage. It had been solemnized in London in July 1915, a mere three months after his first wife's death. Rose Mary was a spinster aged thirty-three, and when she died in 1963 she left a daughter, R. E. Dunham, and a son, George Tyler.

Ford knew little about the Tylers beyond these most basic facts of birth, marriage and death, but he felt sure that if he could find the surviving children of Frederick Tyler's two wives, someone must know what had become of Charles Alexander. Ford could nowhere trace a birth certificate for the Bandmaster himself, so he was prevented from reconstructing the Tyler side of the family.

He was able to unearth a little more about the Webbs. Emma's father, born in 1833, had married Ellen Elliott in London in 1854. From the Pembroke Dock census of 1871 Ford traced four children of the marriage, Emma (born 1861), Rowena (born 1867), Arthur (born 1869 or 1870) and Ada Isobel (born 1877 or 1878). All were born in the little coastal town of Pembroke Dock, where their father, Sidney, worked as a photographer. Ford could not establish whether Arthur or Rowena had married and had children, but Ada Webb married Arthur J. MacDonald, a sergeant in the Royal Artillery in 1897. Although Patricia Roberts had always told Ford that her father was referring to Lady Adelaide FitzGerald when he spoke of his aunt Ada, this was evidently not the case. Ford later found that Ada, after MacDonald's death in 1911, had married Alfred Harden Knock, known as 'Charlie'. This explained the name 'Mrs C. Knock' given as next of kin on Maurice Francis' Canadian Army attestation papers.

After Ada's death, Charlie Knock had married again, and Ford was able to locate both his widow and her daughter, Mrs Farr.

But before Ford could visit Mrs Farr, he received an answer from the National Army Museum. They had been able to identify positively just one of the figures in Maurice Francis' hoard of photographs: it was Bandmaster Frederick Tyler.

Hardly any two families could have been further apart on the social scale than the Tylers and FitzGeralds, a difference which had made research into the former extremely difficult. There was no reference book such as *Burke's* or *Debrett's* in which to look them up, and no written family history. Tyler is not an uncommon name, and though there had been a Colonel Tyler in the King's Royal Rifles, Ford wasn't able to find a relationship with the Bandmaster. Not that peerage books are always accurate; the bulk of the detail is collected from newspaper announcements, proofs being sent to families for verification. If it is imperative for a family to conceal or legitimate a birth or marriage it is done easily enough. It had been done in the case of one of the sixth Duke's uncles, Hubert Duncombe. Although one of Hubert Duncombe's marriages had been mentioned in the American press, there was never any written reference to children; yet Maurice Francis knew of them, and Patricia had met one of Hubert Duncombe's sons by his second wife on her first visit to England in 1971.

Of the four children born to Frederick Tyler by Emma Webb, Edwin died in 1911, Sidney in 1952 and Frederick in 1954, and no record was found in England for Charles Alexander. Sidney left two children, one of whom Ford traced, but he had never heard of his uncle Charles. Frederick, the family historian, had two children, but his daughter was dead, and his son, Reginald, had emigrated to New Zealand with all the papers in his father's possession. Of the Bandmaster's second marriage there were two children, Rose Dunham and George Tyler. If there was any information to be discovered, Ford knew it must come from these two, Reginald Tyler or the widow or daughter of Charlie Knock.

One morning in December 1977 Ford arrived without warning in George Tyler's office. George Tyler was utterly astonished to hear so much about his family that even he didn't know, but he was able to add something to Ford's knowledge of the Bandmaster's long career; he also arranged to accompany Ford on a visit to his sister, Rose Dunham. At last Ford's efforts were beginning to pay off – but, like a pointilliste painting, the subject only coalesced at a distance: looked at closely it was still just a mass of colourful and unconnected points.

George Tyler was only six when his father died but it is doubtful whether, had he been any older, he would have been any the wiser. The Bandmaster had clearly been adept at concealing his past life from his second family.

Frederick John – or Amand – Tyler had first entered the Royal Welch Fusiliers in December 1870 at the age of thirteen. Twelve years later he went to the Royal Military School of Music at Kneller Hall, Twickenham, where the violin was his principal instrument. Less than fifteen months after attending the school he was appointed Bandmaster, the first battalion, the King's Royal Rifle Corps. His swift promotion indicates his remarkable musical ability. Talented musician, outstanding bandmaster and first-class soldier, Frederick Tyler was commended in all reports from his commanding officers for his zeal, efficiency and cheery disposition. He was awarded medals for bravery in the Boer War and the Great War. Well-liked, universally respected, a man who 'often revived the spirits of the men in the trenches', he built up the string section of the first battalion band into the finest in the British

Army. Retiring from the army in 1903 he settled as a music teacher in Monmouth, having enjoyed what appeared to be an exemplary musical career. But there were one or two discordant notes.

Some time after the birth of Edwin, their fourth child, he and his wife parted. Whether this separation was on account of the puerperal mania or the peripatetic nature of military life, George Tyler could not say. But with George Tyler's help Ford was able to obtain the 1891 census for Pembroke Dock. Emma Tyler was listed with her father and one of her children, Charles Alexander. The child's age was stated to be three, although if he was born on 24 January 1887 he should have been four and a half.

That the Bandmaster and his wife did eventually separate is certain. After the Boer War he left the army for the first time. In view of his record and age it was an unexpected decision, and came as a surprise to his superiors. The first the Bandmaster's commanding officer knew of the impending resignation was when he received a letter asking for a reference from one of the people to whom Tyler had applied for a job. Yet he had recently put in for a transfer to the Royal Engineers and appeared to have no intention of leaving the army.

Bandmasters were non-commissioned and messed with the sergeants. Contact with officers, outside routine duties, were normally restricted to regimental occasions. But Frederick Tyler's relations with one officer were much closer than such infrequent and formal contact would account for: this was Brevet Major HRH Prince Christian Victor of Schleswig-Holstein, grandson of Queen Victoria and brother of Princess Louise, a friend of Hermione's.

In a commemorative biography of Prince Christian Victor published in 1903 there was a letter 'from Mr Tyler, Bandmaster to the Prince's Battalion ... who knew him especially well'. In his letter Frederick Tyler laments the loss of many of the Prince's letters when the *Warren Hastings* went down, and describes how the Prince took a great interest in the band and music, giving practical encouragement in the form of 'liberal pecuniary help'. The friendship between the Prince and the Bandmaster seemed to extend beyond music, as Tyler wrote:

> When the siege of Ladysmith was raised and he rode in to see us, his first question was 'Where is Mr Tyler?' ... His kindness to me and my children was that of a true friend. His was a kind disposition, and though poles apart socially, on one side the rough soldier and on the other the cultured Prince, he was the best friend I ever had ... Personally I was stupefied [by the news of his death] and some old hands, though feeling the shock keenly, condoled me, knowing I had lost a true friend.

George Tyler could not account for his father's friendship with Prince Christian Victor, except perhaps for the unusual character of the regiment. Formed in North America in 1755 as the 60th Regiment of Foot, it was said that 'they have become one of the most exclusive family regiments in the military world. No one could hope to become an officer in the 60th without close family connections.' The FitzGeralds had connections with the regiment, and Lord Frederick and Lord Walter had served in it during the 1880s. Of Frederick Tyler's sons, four served in the regiment; his son Frederick was offered, but turned down, a commission during the Great War. The only son not to join was Charles Alexander.

The closeness of the Bandmaster's connection with Prince Christian Victor was later confirmed by his grandson Reginald Tyler, who Ford finally tracked down in New Zealand. Among the few heirlooms which passed to Reginald was a hawthorn

walking-stick with a silver band inscribed 'HRH Prince
Christian Victor – presented by HRH Christian to F. Tyler BM, I
KRR, October 1902'. As Prince Christian Victor died in 1900
this was probably presented to the Bandmaster by the Prince's
mother, Princess Helena, when he stayed at Cumberland
Lodge in October 1902 – the telegram from her to the Bandmaster's commanding officer asking that he be allowed to stay
a night there is still in George Tyler's possession.

However, when the Bandmaster left the army he went to
lodge with a family named Wood, a mother and daughter. He
was an upright, spruce, jovial figure in his late forties, with an
interesting and distinguished past. He had travelled widely
and was one of the survivors of the wreck of the *Warren Hastings*,
in which he had lost most of his worldly goods. He made quite
an impact on the Wood family. In 1909 Mrs Wood's daughter,
Rose Mary, gave birth to a daughter, Rose, known as 'Nin'. The
ex-Bandmaster rejoined the army in 1914 and, in his late fifties,
was on active service in the trenches: he was particularly good at
raising morale among the raw recruits. In 1915 he returned to
marry Rose and in 1920 a second child, George, was born.

Nin Dunham had very fond memories of her father. She had
been very close to him and still possessed many family photographs. As far as she could remember, Charlie had disappeared to America around 1910, though she clearly recalled
a surprise visit he had made to his father during the Great War.
She even had a photograph which commemorated the
occasion. Standing behind her and half-brother Sidney stood a
moustachioed figure sporting a Canadian uniform. It was Patricia's father. Among his possessions 'Maurice Francis' had a
similar photograph showing himself and a young girl – unmistakably Nin – and when Patricia had asked her father who the
little girl was, he had replied, 'The photographer's daughter.'
According to Nin, at the time of his visit Charlie was on his way

to Shorncliffe Barracks in Kent, and it was probably in 1916. A couple of years later he dropped in again on his return from fighting in France. He told the family he had changed his name to FitzGerald, and demanded that any letters should be addressed to him by that name; he seemed to be very comfortably provided for from an unidentified source. Nin never saw him again after that second visit and thought he married a film star after he returned to America.

Bandmaster Tyler had never been one for reminiscing. Whenever Nin or George asked him about his life before they were born (he was in his fifties when he married their mother) he simply avoided the question – a trait his son Charlie seemed to have inherited. The Bandmaster was not easily riled, but Nin remembered that when Charlie appeared just after the war using the name FitzGerald, her father had stormed out of the room. The Bandmaster's son Frederick had also been present, and asked someone what the matter was. 'Oh, it's Charlie,' the reply came. 'He could cause a lot of trouble using that name.'

Whenever Nin had listened to her half-brothers Frederick and Sidney discussing their childhood, they spoke of three boys, the third being Edwin. George Tyler showed Ford two letters to his father which referred to 'both your boys' and 'both your little boys'. Nobody talked about Charlie, the only son on the 1891 census for Pembroke Dock.

Finally, Ford called on Mrs Farr, daughter of Alfred 'Charlie' Knock by his second marriage. She knew little of the Tyler family, though she did recall going with her father to a cowboy film in the 1930s; one of the characters in it was called either Tom or Charlie Tyler and her father remarked that he was 'a sort of cousin of yours'. Mrs Farr's mother, widow of Charlie Knock, added her tiny contribution when, on being asked about the Tylers, she responded without hesitation, 'Oh yes, there was some terrible scandal about a bandmaster.'

It seemed to Ford that he had at last solved the mystery, or at least untangled its central knot. As a young man Charlie Tyler had gone to America, at a date as yet unknown, and for unexplained reasons. Subsequently he had changed his name, pretending by a kind of double bluff that Charlie Tyler was a friend whose name he had borrowed. First he became Francis FitzGerald, then Francis Maurice, later Maurice Francis, finally, to his family, just Maurice. With his new identity came a new past.

Ford's opinion was that Maurice Francis had woven a story around the Leinsters which was not in fact based on that family at all, but on the Tylers. There were in the Tyler family four boys, there was an elder brother Frederick (though he was no invalid), there was a brother who had been killed while in the army, there was a brother 'Ted' and an Aunt Ada. A military connection did exist between the Tylers and FitzGeralds, though the Bandmaster and the FitzGerald uncles had not served in the same battalion. These extraordinary coincidences between the two families obscured many of the discrepancies in Charlie Tyler's stories.

But the discovery of the real identity of Patricia's father still left several questions unresolved. What was Charlie Tyler's origin, how random were his motives, and how had he learned so much about the sixth Duke of Leinster?

From what he heard from Nin Dunham, Ford inferred that Charlie had grown up apart from his brothers. Frederick and Sidney had never mentioned Charlie; he had not attended the same school or joined the regiment. When he turned up on the Bandmaster's doorstep it was the first that Nin – ostensibly his half-sister – had ever heard of him; he was the only one of

Emma Tyler's children to appear on the Pembroke Dock census. That he called himself a FitzGerald in the hearing of the Bandmaster, thereby incensing an otherwise even-tempered man to sudden fury, suggested that he was in some way a FitzGerald. It was, after all, one thing to call himself Fitz-Gerald in America where people were ignorant of his identity, but quite another to do so in front of the man supposed – and possibly paid – to be his father. The Bandmaster's mother-in-law had reacted immediately and nervously to Charlie using the name, as if aware of a scandal about to break. It is unlikely that the Bandmaster's sudden rage was that of a father distressed at his son's rejecting the family surname. It was possible that when in 1916 Charlie had given the name of his aunt, his mother's sister, as his next of kin he was bringing into the open the fact that the Bandmaster was not his father. Similarly, the name Frederick Charles FitzGerald, which he gave on his first marriage certificate as being that of his father, may have contained some truth; Charlie may have been a natural son of either Lord Frederick or Lord Charles Fitz-Gerald. And, if he knew the rumours concerning the seventh Duke's parentage, he might have felt that he had as much right to be Duke of Leinster after 1922 as the man who succeeded.

In 1886 the first battalion of the King's Royal Rifles were stationed in Dublin. For some of the time both Lord Charles and Lord Frederick were there; Lord Frederick also lived at Parkhurst on the Isle of Wight, where Charlie was born. The circumstances surrounding Lord Charles' departure from Ireland in 1887 are somewhat vague; Charlie told his children that Lord Charles left under a bit of a cloud. There was also the choice of names: Ford found no other Tyler called Charles, but both the fourth Duke and his fifth son bore that name. Moreover, Charlie Tyler as an old man bore the most extraordinary resemblance to the fourth Duke. He could not have been one of Hermione's sons if he was born in January 1887, for she could not have managed to give birth to one in January and another in March that year, but he could have been born to her in February 1886. That Charlie's birth was registered just one day after the birth of the sixth Duke was probably coincidental; if the Bandmaster had not been with his wife at the time of the child's conception there may have been a confrontation between them causing a delay in registration. On the other hand, Charlie may not have been registered until the fifth Duke and Duchess had produced a legitimate heir, whose birthright could have been jeopardized by Charlie's existence. Certainly it is curious that on the Pembroke Dock census of 1891 it is Charlie and not the youngest child who was with his mother.

Lord Charles suffered none of the social inhibitions of the FitzGeralds of his generation; he gave up his title when he emigrated. If he was Charlie's father it might explain why Charlie went to Australia in 1907, and why Lord Charles never returned to England, where the family considered him a black sheep. Reginald Tyler, the Bandmaster's grandson, contributed something to Charlie Tyler's Australian connection. He wrote:

> I have been told that he came over with the Australian Light Horse as a rough riding sergeant early in the war, took his discharge in England and then sailed for America where he rode for the film industry under the name of Cowboy Charlie. My mother once referred to him as the black sheep of the family, but my father demurred, and that is about all I can recall about uncle Charles.

This rather conflicted with the results of Ford's research, though it was in the Australian Light Horse that Charles Otho (born in 1895), one of Lord Charles' sons, served during the Great War. But, if Lord Charles already owned to one son called Charles – albeit illegitimate – would he call another by the same name?

The possibility that Lord Charles was Charlie Tyler's father was supported by Colonel John Moloney. A grandson of Lord Charles, he had done much of the Australian research, canvassing every member of the Australian branch of the FitzGeralds for photographs and letters, as most of Lord Charles' papers had gone astray. When this theory was later presented to the eighth Duke it was readily accepted. He said it was common knowledge in the family that Lord Charles had conducted a liaison with 'a Miss Tyler' on the passage to India.

11

Missing Links

IT was still a mystery whence Charlie had acquired his extensive knowledge of FitzGerald affairs. It seemed probable that he had at least visited Carton, and this was confirmed by a totally independent source. Shortly before his death, Patricia's father had conferred at length with a priest called Liam Toohey. Patricia was convinced the priest had been given a deathbed message for the seventh Duke. Now back in America, McGuire finally located Toohey, who denied that he was given any such mission, but was sure that 'Maurice Francis' had been to Carton. Father Toohey had trained at the seminary at Maynooth and had frequently been to the house and grounds, and conversations with 'Maurice Francis' had convinced him that he knew it well. It was almost fifty years since Charlie had left England, yet his memories seemed real enough to the priest.

At the same time, Ford went to Pembroke Dock to find out more about Charlie's early life there. He visited the old Webb house and was told that Emma had another sister who Ford had not heard of before. She was called Ella, and had been dead for twenty years, but her son Jimmy lived in Birmingham.

Jimmy Brown described how he and his mother had moved to Pembroke Dock to help Emma and her octogenarian father,

Sidney Webb. Emma was failing and not entirely sane. Jimmy had known most of the family, Ada and her two husbands, Arthur and Rowena. He had also met Charlie.

During the First World War a dapper figure in Canadian uniform had arrived at the house. He was suave and well educated. He told them he was acting in films with Douglas Fairbanks and Mary Pickford, but no one believed him. His mother had died about a year before. Charlie was using the name FitzGerald, but was thought of as Charlie Tyler. Jimmy never saw him again. He told Ford that Richard Edge, Edwin's murderer, had been exiled from the country in the interests of the good name of the King's Royal Rifles. This treatment offered one explanation for the absence of records in the regimental archives covering Edwin's death and the subsequent trial.

Several people had now told Ford of Charlie's apparent affluence, and Patricia remembered her mother talking of a large allowance. Patricia spoke of her own earliest memories of a luxurious life, and that this came to an end during the mid 1920s. The source of this money might explain with which of the FitzGerald family Charlie was in contact, though whether the money was a paternal contribution or a payment to keep Charlie quiet at a time when the new Duke, the FitzGeralds and Mallaby-Deeleys wanted to avoid scandal at all costs was impossible to discover.

Edward Pierce, whom Charlie had met in early days in Meeteetsee, remembered him as a fine gentleman, polished, honourable, wearing a handsome stetson and taking alcohol only occasionally. Pierce remained friends with Charlie for the rest of his life and was sure that his friend could never lie. Charlie told Pierce that he had previously occupied some 'high position' and Pierce thought he may have received sums of money from abroad from time to time; Charlie's father was an officer stationed in England or India, and his family came from Ireland. Pierce's mother told her son that Charlie was 'no ordinary person' and that his family was connected with royalty. All these things could, with little exaggeration, be said of the Tylers. Pierce never heard the dukedom mentioned until after his friend's death in 1967.

McGuire traced three sisters named Bennett who lived in Meeteetsee and confirmed that Charlie had been there as early as 1910. He did not appear to have any money other than what he earned, but he did file for some grazing land, which wasn't very valuable, while he was living there. The Bennetts remembered him always as the perfect gentleman; he had also given a definite impression of having a blood connection with royalty. He seemed regretful about leaving England, but only mentioned one brother, whose death occurred while he was staying with the Bennetts; they remembered him receiving photographs of a grand military funeral. The third Bennett sister remembered his confiding to her that he was a duke, and a year or so after he had become close to the family he said his name was FitzGerald, not Tyler. This antedated by some time any public use of the name.

Cupples Scudder first saw Charlie riding bucking broncos for Buffalo Bill Cody in the 101 Wild West Show in 1913. No records of that period now exist; the show came to an end that year and Charlie left to train polo ponies at the St Louis Country Club. In 1914 and 1915 Charlie took Scudder on long trips with horses and packs. On the 1915 trip they camped in Yellowstone Park for five weeks, and while they were there Charlie had an accident. Scudder's version was rather different from Patricia's: Charlie was out roping a horse, lost his temper and caught the rope round the horse's stomach, causing the horse to fall on top of him, crushing Charlie's head. Scudder took him to hospital where he was unconscious or delirious for the best part of ten days. Scudder then did not see his friend for some thirty years; in 1944 they met again and Charlie managed one of Scudder's ranches for him.

Scudder belonged to a long-established American family, with the accompanying nose for social pretension. He believed Charlie, although he said he was a 'peculiar man', and avoided questions about his origins. Scudder gathered that Charlie had estates in Ireland but, wishing to remain in America, had turned everything over to his brother. While Charlie was living near Meeteetsee he shared a log cabin with three roughnecks who, he told Scudder, were supported by the money he received from England. Charlie had poor eyesight and spoke beautiful English; he gave the impression of being highly educated. Scudder, although he did not see Charlie for thirty years after his accident, felt that he must have sustained brain damage, though his instant physical recovery was astonishing. It must have been, for otherwise he could not have been accepted by the Canadian Overseas Expeditionary Force less than a year afterwards.

In Wyoming Charlie had certainly picked a fertile ground for weaving romances, for it was a region which abounded with expatriates of dubious antecedents. In the 1870s Cheyenne had, in but a few years, become one of the most cosmopolitan towns in America; the Cheyenne Club buzzed with excited talk of potential, opportunity and impracticable ideas. But by the end of the 1880s boom-time was over and many of the adventurers went home, leaving the real cowboys behind them to a life they had found both compelling and disconcerting. Their dusty glamour provided stories for generations. Much of this had changed by the time Charlie arrived, but the things he did and claimed to have done – working for Buffalo Bill, training polo ponies, co-ordinating battle scenes for *The Charge of the Light Brigade*, a stuntsman for westerns, presenting a stetson to the Prince of Wales, meeting Theodore Roosevelt – all reflect the highly-coloured, backward-looking imagination of the Bandmaster's son who, rather than live out a life as an NCO, crossed the Atlantic in search of adventure. He even said he had been a member of the Cheyenne Club, which had closed decades before he was there. Charlie's horsemanship was superb and there were no doubts about his courage; he received the Military Medal and Bar. All this was real. But it is ironic that in the self-styled land of opportunity he should have become so dependent on a baroque dream of lost grandeur.

This was perhaps the real explanation for Charlie's stories. Nothing he said suggested that he was mad in the traditional manner of lunatics who believe they are Napoleon; on the contrary, everyone was impressed by his easy-going charm, courtesy, modesty and humour. In any case, it is one thing to assume the role of a safely-dead historical figure, quite another to claim to be a specific contemporary duke.

The story of the dukedom may have started as a sort of joke after he came out of hospital, but with his English accent and manners one or two people believed him; after a time he was hooked on his own bait. There were so many coincidences between the two families that the line between them became blurred over the years. Except for one Bennett sister being told in 'about 1912' (she could not be positive about the year) that his real name was FitzGerald, there was no reason to believe that he had used the name before his accident.

But Patricia remained as convinced as ever of her father's stories, and to prove it she at last let Ford listen to a tape of her father's voice. It was just a senseless babble of voices, and confirmed Ford's doubts about the transcripts she had sent him earlier. She then produced a large box of Eleanor Gough's papers which had 'suddenly' been found, and a number of photographs, including one of the eighth Duke as a boy and another of Lord Frederick. Patricia refused to disclose the source of these photographs, which were originals, but said simply that they had belonged to her father. They may have come from among the FitzGerald effects at Hearst's castle in California. Finally she announced that there was a trunk of her father's papers in the attic of her house which she had not had time to examine since her father's death a decade before. After the years Ford had spent corresponding with Patricia, basing his researches on the information she had supplied, his exasperation was understandable.

Patricia also wondered if she might in the past have been too hasty in condemning a pet theory long held by her sister Theresa. This, of all things, was that her father had not been Maurice at all, but Lord Desmond! No life could be more straightforward, no death more reliably witnessed or precisely documented than Lord Desmond's. There were no lost medical records, no sceptical pall-bearers, no conflicting accounts. To believe that Charlie Tyler was Lord Desmond demanded an almost supernatural suspension of disbelief and an astonishing feat of legerdemain to explain the public death in France. Nonetheless, to substantiate this extravagant notion she set about compiling yet another massive dossier of evidence and sent it to McGuire and Ford marked 'highly confidential'.

The Desmond theory did produce one curious fact. Charlie had spoken of having been forbidden to marry his cousin, Marian Beckett. Marian Frances Theresa was the daughter of Hermione's niece, Mabel Duncombe, and it was after her that Theresa said she was named. Marian was now dead, but Ford traced her sister, who told him that Marian had been in love with Lord Desmond.

The idea that Patricia's father was a Tyler was vehemently denied, though she accepted that the FitzGeralds and the Tylers knew each other. The idea, she said, was based only on the testimony of Nin Dunham and others who had been only children at the time of Charlie's wartime visits to the Bandmaster's family. Leonard too was reluctant to believe that he was Charlie Tyler's son, but relieved that the whole business of the claim was over, for he was still far from well. It simply saddened him that the name he would bequeath to his sons had no connection with his family history.

Charlie Tyler's mind had worked in riddles and what he said became a series of conundrums which his audience could only have cracked with the truth. There were endless opportunities for misunderstandings, jumping to wrong conclusions, *double entendres*. Coincidence had supported Charlie's story strongly, apocryphal or not. His birth *was* registered one day after the birth of the sixth Duke; there was a Tyler at school with the sixth Duke; Charlie was married one day after the order in lunacy was taken out against the sixth Duke. Patricia herself had acknowledged more than once that her father was a bit of a tease. He was indeed, but on a scale of which she had no idea. Towards the end of his life it was beyond his control. Through all the elaborate pretence ran a vein of ambiguity; references to the Tylers were assumed to be references to the FitzGeralds and the half-truth produced a garbled authenticity. Shortly before his death, Patricia's father said that soon the title would no longer be rightfully his. Though he kept up the fiction to the last, the title could never have been rightfully his; at his death, the fantasy and the fantastic obligations it imposed, would be over – at any rate for him.

12

The Tin Trunk

NOW it was clear that Leonards father was Charlie Tyler it seemed reasonable to assume that the inmate of Craighouse was Maurice, sixth Duke of Leinster. Charlie Tyler had lied so much that there did not seem much cause to believe his story of the fourth boy. Ford wondered if Charlie Tyler had been speaking of himself when he had spoken of a fourth boy, especially as he had been uncertain whether the child was a brother or a cousin. The Tyler brothers had never mentioned Charlie as being part of their childhood, and a feeling of alienation from his first family could have driven a sensitive and histrionic child to seek security in the fiction of another.

If it hadn't been for Charlie Tyler and his claim, no one would ever have doubted the identity of the man in Craighouse. The whole life of this man was deliberately clouded. There were unanswered questions about his general health, his epilepsy, his education, his travels, the reasons for his incarceration in a lunatic asylum; even photographs caused confusion. There was much inaccurate information printed about the children of the fifth Duke, not merely in the press but in publications where it was least excusable. There were discrepancies about his age throughout his life, and even on his grave. It was odd that in each case the error gave him an extra year – the year which could have rendered him Hermione's dead daughter.

Only in the light of Charlie's stories could all the inconsistencies be interpreted as a single conspiracy. The sixth Duke's life, publicly viewed, was so largely composed of columnists' fictions, romantic yearnings and the common fantasy of how a duke ought to comfort himself, that even without the help of Charlie Tyler mistakes had crept in. The story of the twentieth-century Leinsters was already peculiar; certainly no other British ducal family had suffered such reverses of fortune in Charlie Tyler's lifetime.

The real Maurice, Marquess of Kildare, born on 1 March 1887, who became Duke on his father's death in 1893, had probably been delicate in some unspecified nineteenth-century way, perhaps victim to the childish form of epilepsy. As often happens, this may have disappeared before adolescence, only to return in more acute form after he left Eton. He was put under the care of a personal physician – this is a clear indication of how ill the Duke must have been – and his role in public life as the premier nobleman of Ireland steadily reduced. The state of his health was clouded with euphemism, and his committal to Craighouse was concealed as foreign travel or living in Ireland. His brothers and cousins may have visited him occasionally, but until his brother's bankruptcy hearing in 1919 his very existence was hidden from the world. No family cares to display insanity; rather than risk stirring up old rumours the FitzGeralds organized the quietest possible funeral when the sixth Duke died, with the briefest announcement of his death, a terse inscription on his tombstone, and a handful of people at the funeral. Ireland was on the verge of civil war; the FitzGeralds' life and livelihood was crumbling round them. They were tenants on estates which had been theirs for over six centuries – the inheritance they had zealously guarded throughout the sixth Duke's life had been sold for a mere £67,500 to a parvenu from London.

Ford knew how easy it was for a researcher to become hypnotized by the written word, by dates and press reports. Documents are his essential; they reveal information which is the researcher's raw material. But they leave out a whole dimension in their portrayal of human affairs – the quirks and foibles, the vanities and fears, the impulses and fallibilities of individuals.

Ford never saw the Craighouse records but towards the end of 1977 he received a letter from Mr Ian Davie which appeared to confirm that the inmate of Craighouse was the sixth Duke.

I well remember my father telling me how he and several of his contemporaries would earn pocket money, as medical students at Edinburgh University, by becoming paid companions to the Duke during vacations.

Whether this involved trips abroad I cannot say for certain, but it did involve my father in several Pirandello-like situations, such as reviewing imaginary troops and reading out menus to barmecide feasts. And it occurs to me that the Court Circular entry dated 11 March 1910 [which stated that the Duke 'will shortly arrive in England from abroad'] is perhaps explained as an attempt either to humour the deluded Duke if he had not been abroad, or to gratify his sense of ducal importance if in fact he had been abroad ... It was probably inserted by one of the Duke's 'companions', as I remember hearing something to that effect. The impression that I gained from my father's reminiscences was that the sixth Duke was infinitely suggestible and totally deluded (though I can't say which was cause and which effect), but he would seem to have been courteous, good-humoured, and my father would describe him as a 'typical Etonian' – in point of good manners, I presume – however dangerous he may have been in his distraught condition . . . As the sixth Duke was an almost legendary figure in psychiatric circles I would not be surprised if a case history had been published in the professional journals of the period . . . though the subject of such a case history would not be identified by name, internal evidence should make such an identification possible.

But no detailed case history has been located.

In pursuit of other records on the Duke, an MP who was making enquiries on James Arthur's behalf visited the House of Commons library in order to look at their file on the Leinster dukedom. As all enquiries of this type are considered confidential he was surprised to receive a stern letter from the Lord Chancellor's Office demanding to know why he was interested. Although a desire to meet the MP and discuss the matter was expressed, this was rescinded when an appointment was sought.

McGuire found further corroboration for the lunacy of the sixth Duke from a man named William Synott living in San Francisco. He had been a pantry boy at Carton in about 1923; he was only there for a year, as the staff were cut back after Lord Frederick's death. Synott remembered passing the time of day with a parlourmaid who had idly mentioned the late Duke's madness and that he had had to live in Edinburgh.

But for James Arthur the mystery was not at an end. He still believed the inmate had been the girl born in 1886, although this idea still left the problem of the second son, if he were not Charlie Tyler. James Arthur could not understand Patricia's motive in having the records sealed; they were on very friendly terms. He spoke to his MP, who put the request to the Under-Secretary of State for Scotland but, after extensive enquiries, it was decided that it was best for all concerned that the Craig-house file remained private.

It was another three years before the identity of the Craighouse inmate was finally settled. In the spring of 1980 the eighth Duke had returned to him several tin trunks of deeds which had been lost for years following many changes of family lawyers. One of the trunks was marked 'Maurice, Duke of Leinster' and contained correspondence, bills, accounts and other documents relating to the thirteen years between the Duke's majority and his death.

It also contained the first clear account of the events preceding the young Duke's arrival at Craighouse. From letters between Dr Pollock and the FitzGeralds' family solicitor, Mr Johnson, it was obvious that in the summer of 1909 the sixth Duke's behaviour was causing increasing alarm. Nonetheless, a cruise was planned on the yacht *Laranda*, and a holiday in North Berwick was arranged until the yacht should be ready. It was in North Berwick, on 11 June 1909, that the Duke, having 'for the past five days laboured under intense mental excitement', tried to kill himself, his valet and his personal physician.

It is not difficult to imagine the horror and alarm which must have greeted news of the Duke's sudden violent outburst. For some years it had been possible to humour him by constant travel and the presence of a concerned companion with similar interests. Away from England, perhaps travelling incognito, it had been possible to keep the press at bay and all its enquiries regarding the Duke's plans for the future, possibilities of marriage, and his role in Irish affairs. Now, as a result of his sudden frenzy – it is unclear whether he tried to kill himself first and attacked his valet and doctor only when they tried to stop him, or that, having failed to kill them, he attempted to do away with himself – the terrible threat of a public trial and massive press coverage presented itself. The only alternative was the Duke's speedy incarceration in an asylum.

As soon as Lord Frederick heard of the attack he sent Dr Clouston to see the Duke. In his report, which formed part of the Petition to the Sheriff to grant an order for the reception of the Duke into an asylum, Dr Clouston wrote:

> I am of the opinion that he is of unsound mind and understanding, under many insane delusions viz. that Pollock, his valet and other persons present are trying to injure him. He is also dangerously suicidal and homicidal, having inflicted a serious wound on his throat and several other wounds on his chest and arm as well as having seriously assaulted Dr Pollock.

Dr Robertson, Physician-Superintendent of the Royal Edinburgh Asylum, made similar comments in his affidavit. Robertson explained to the Duke that the management of his affairs should now be placed on a proper footing, to which end the Petition was served as a necessary preliminary. 'I thereupon read him the whole Petition,' Dr Robertson wrote to Lord Frederick, '... he listened to it all without being upset or annoyed in the least and he stated that you had helped to look after his estates since he had succeeded and that he hoped you would continue to do so. He has taken no further interest in the Petition and has never spoken about it but has devoted his attention almost entirely to naval questions.' A few days later the Duke's attitude had changed. On 1 July Clouston wrote that the Duke 'is now talking of "having his side of the question heard" and does not in the least realize the seriousness of his acts at North Berwick'. On 14 July Pollock wrote to Mr Johnson: 'I am sorry to say that he has had a twist of a mental nature which will I fear prove permanent. He still believes he was justified in acting as he did because he was persecuted.'

The examination was set to take place at the Red Lion Hotel, Berwick-on-Tweed, on 23 July 1909. One of the best known British neurologists, Dr Alexander Bruce, was retained as an independent doctor to act on the Duke's behalf, but the out-come must have been certain beforehand. The Duke obviously found his aunt (and other guardian), Lady Cynthia Graham, the most sympathetic of his family, and it would appear he had some influence over her. 'Lady Cynthia is so emotional,' wrote Lord Frederick to Mr Johnson after the examination, 'that she wishes to act always on the spur of the moment. One cannot say to her, that the matter is entirely out of her hands, in any case. So it is well the matter is under the control of the authorities.' And the following day, 30 July: 'The Duke writes to Lady Cynthia complaining about the place and the sight of the inmates . . . If you see the Master in Lunacy you might tell him how impossible it would be for him to be in any way safe here [Carton], from your knowledge of the place; so it need not be thought about.' Nor did Lord Frederick like 'to have the responsibility of a private house arrangement'.

As early as 16 June, a few days after the North Berwick incident and well before the Examination, terms for the Duke's residence at Craighouse as an 'extraordinary patient and boarder' had been arranged. They were to vary little for the rest of his life. For £2,500 per annum the Duke enjoyed ex-clusive use of the Bungalow, a semi-detached villa some fifty yards from the main building, special board, the service of a doctor, the exclusive service of five attendants, one of whom was the Duke's recently-assaulted valet, and the use of a car-riage and pair.

The Duke's friend and physician, Dr Pollock, was deeply

shocked and unnerved by the whole episode. 'I am trying to induce sleep here by means of physical weariness from hard exercise,' he wrote to the FitzGeralds' family solicitor, Mr Johnson, on 3 July; a few weeks later he said he was better but still found the nightmares rather worrying. Dr Pollock's position became somewhat awkward after his charge's incarceration; because of his proximity the Duke had cast his erstwhile friend as a persecutor. Originally hired as a permanent private physician to the Duke, Pollock had come to a more formal arrangement on the Duke's coming of age. He had received an annual salary plus expenses and the promise of a lump sum of £5,000 in the event of the Duke's death or termination of the agreement, provided the Duke did not die through Pollock's failure to perform his duties. They had lived at 140 Earls Court Road in a rented house, but this would be needed no longer. The *Laranda*, fitted out at great expense for the Duke's cruise, was cancelled.

Pollock was now forbidden by the family to live at Craighouse because of the Duke's new attitude towards him, and he was obliged to find lodgings in Edinburgh. His devotion to the sixth Duke never wavered: 'Apart from one or two near relatives I am really the only friend he has, and I am sure something such as occurred would have happened sooner or later had it not been for his liking for me. If this were destroyed his recovery might be hindered.' He wrote to Mr Johnson on 27 July:

I may tell you that the medical impression is that he will sooner or later commit suicide wherever he is but that the chances of his doing this are very much less where he is than in an outside establishment. Of course there is another point. There is no Coroner in Scotland and all the abominable publicity attached to his court. But still, we must not anticipate such a catastrophe. Poor boy, it's a terrible ending for a short and sharp life's tragedy.

The Duke's future was indeed bleak. He remained moody and unpredictable, given to long periods of total silence, when he would not eat, alternating with bursts of manic activity. In 1914 Dr Robertson wrote, 'He does curling, hockey, music . . . they provided a piano fitted with organ pedals' (to encourage him to think he might play the organ at Carton) but his eyesight was failing. In 1915 the Duke wrote pathetically to 'My dear uncle Freddie . . . as regards self one feels inclined to leave and get hold of some work elsewhere; one could be happy at one's own home. . . . Hoping to meet you either in London or perhaps on the way there.' Having his portrait painted was one of the few things the Duke enjoyed. He got on well with the artist, Fiddes Watt, who received 150 guineas for the painting. It disappeared after the Duke's death; it may have been given to Pollock as a memento, if he needed one, of his years of service, but it wasn't mentioned in Pollock's will. It may have been sold in one of the bankruptcy auctions at Carton.

With the outbreak of war the asylum was drained of its able-bodied staff. Old men might not be up to supervising the Duke, and Pollock was no help as the Duke continued to think the doctor was persecuting him. Relays of students were necessary to keep him company, as Ford learned from Ian Davie, and Dr Robertson wrote to the FitzGeralds' solicitors anxiously requesting a £500 increase in the Duke's fees.

For the FitzGeralds things must have appeared pretty hopeless. Early in the war Pollock wrote on hearing of an injury sustained by Lord Desmond: 'I am glad that Desmond's wound is no worse. Personally I feel thankful that he is not in the middle of it and may be kept out of it for good. With Ed. as successor things would be too dreadful.' But Desmond returned to the front where he was to die, and it was Edward who was invalided home. Among the letters there is a passing reference suggesting that Edward may have visited his brother in Scotland, and that an unpleasant scene took place between them. After the war there was not much correspondence; there are entries in the account books to show the Duke was still alive, and some details concerning funeral arrangements when he died in February 1922.

If the sixth Duke did die of unnatural causes the circumstances were covered up very quickly; Lord Frederick signed the death certificate within a day of the Duke's demise, and there was no post mortem. Despite the pall-bearers' reported disquiet over the contents of the coffin there seemed to Ford no justifiable grounds for applying for an exhumation order.

13

Staking a Claim

PUBLIC cupidity keeps fraud alive. In 1867, a hundred years before Charles Alexander Tyler died under the name Maurice Francis FitzGerald in California, it became known in England that a man had appeared in answer to a newspaper advertisement claiming to be the long-lost Roger Tichborne. The heir to the Tichborne baronetcy and estates had been given up as drowned off the coast of South America thirteen years earlier; now he returned from Australia. Lady Tichborne recognized him as her son; the rest of the family repudiated him as an impostor; the public, captivated, became passionate partisans and the controversy raged throughout the country, in and out of the courts for over ten years. 'The Claimant', as he was always known, was eventually gaoled for fourteen years for perjury. *The Standard* described him as the 'most daring swindler of our time, the most audacious rascal that ever devised a scheme to delude a nation, the most consummate perjurer, and hypocrite, if not worse, that our age has known' and the *Pall Mall Gazette* regretted that he was not hanged.

After the trial Joseph Brown QC published a pamphlet on the case. In it he said:

It does not seem creditable either to the British public that it should have been so long in opening its eyes, or to the courts of justice that they should have required such an enormous expense of time and money to expose such a gross fraud.... So far from the Tichborne Case being a novelty ... whenever a prince or king has disappeared under mysterious circumstances, an impostor has generally appeared to counterfeit him with amazing effrontery, tempted by personal likeness, by the support of dupes and interested persons, and by the great prize of a kingdom. There appears to be a strange temptation to human nature to practise impostures of this kind ... but when a man openly personates another who has not been heard of for many years, and lays claim to the property of the lost man, the risk of detection must needs be so great, looking at the persons interested in exposing the fraud, that there must be some extraordinary temptation to induce a man to brave it, and one would expect such a case to be a rare occurrence. On the contrary. Firstly the prize to be won is very great and should he fail yet a needy and desperate adventurer will have been the winner by the game, for he will have had the satisfaction of making himself famous, of becoming a popular hero, and of making a crowd of dupes and fanatical followers, who will probably have supported him in ease and luxury for years before the final detection, and will even continue their faith and bounty after he has been exposed.

Human nature does not change. The modern impostor may risk a swift unmasking, but he also stands to profit as much from being caught as not. This is an age of celebrities, of people famous only for being famous. Many admire the nerve of the man prepared to chance the penalties of the law.

In his study of impostors Egon Larsen even went so far as to write:

> The impostor in particular fulfils a most wholesome func-
> tion, that of social criticism. He reveals his fellow-men's
> failings and vices by using them as the very basis of his
> schemes, showing them in outsize proportions in himself
> or, more frequently, in his victims ... to those of us who
> want to use their eyes and ears, the impostor teaches a
> beneficial lesson; he may not be a better man than his
> victims but he certainly invites more sympathy.

Charlie Tyler does not invite sympathy, although the tales
he spun his family were evidently in earnest. He seemed to
know much that was not generally available, but his constantly
changing mixture of half-truths and deliberate lies was bound
to cause confusion. He juxtaposed names and events in the
Tyler family with those in the FitzGerald family, so that when
he seemed to be talking about one he was in fact referring to the
other. After fifty years of deception he had probably come to
believe all he said. It is certain that the man who died in
California in 1967 was not Maurice Francis FitzGerald, for
that person died aged six days old; as Charles Alexander Tyler
his identity has been established beyond reasonable doubt.

Similarly, there are no adequate grounds for believing that
the occupant of the Bungalow, Morningside Drive, Edinburgh,
was other than Maurice, sixth Duke of Leinster. True, much
confusion still surrounds this figure. There are the incorrect
ages on the Duke's death certificate and the 1902 shipping lists
for his voyage to Australia; there is the letter in the Craighouse
records from Lady Cynthia Graham insisting that he should
not be given an address he should have known well; there is the
seventh Duke's insistence to his wife that his brother was
definitely not insane and the pall-bearers' comments about the

sixth Duke's coffin. There was also the local gossip about a fourth boy, on which the wills of the fourth Duke and Duchess and Kilkea Parish Records might have thrown some light if they had still existed.

Charlie Tyler's blood relation to the FitzGeralds cannot be dismissed out of hand. It would explain his intimate knowledge of the family's affairs and the money he apparently had as a young man which could not have come from the Tylers. In his old age he bore a striking resemblance to the fourth Duke, whose Christian name he shared. The battalion in which the Bandmaster served was stationed in Dublin in 1886 when Charlie was conceived; Lord Charles FitzGerald, a brother of the fifth Duke, was there at the same time and shortly afterwards left Ireland, never to return. The eighth Duke has spoken of a rumour that Lord Charles had an affair with a 'Miss Tyler' in India, where the Bandmaster was stationed at various times. Lord Walter and Lord Frederick also served with the King's Royal Rifles, and Lord Frederick was living on the Isle of Wight around the time of Charlie's birth there. If Charlie thought he was an illegitimate FitzGerald it might account for a belief that he was entitled to more recognition from that family than he received, but any suggestion of an 'abdication agreement' was pure fancy and weakened his story considerably. He could not claim to be both Maurice, sixth Duke of Leinster (abdicated), as Dermot Morrah was told, and Maurice, rightful Duke after 1922.

Little appears to have been known of Charlie within the Tyler family. When he arrived on their doorstep during the Great War it was the first Nin Tyler, his half-sister, had heard of him. He was not brought up with the other Tyler boys, and he could not be traced at any school they attended. He did not join the King's Royal Rifles, and it is not known whether he joined any other British regiments before serving with the

Canadian Expeditionary Overseas Force; he listed two regiments on his attestation paper, both of which have no records of the pre-Great War period. The Bandmaster's fury on hearing Charlie call himself FitzGerald, and the subsequent remark that he 'could get into a lot of trouble using that name' has been affirmed, but it is not known whether the Bandmaster's resignation from the army in 1903 and his reticence on the subject of his marriage to Emma Tyler are in any way connected with Charlie.

Even if Charlie Tyler was an illegitimate member of the FitzGerald family it does not explain the obvious lies he told his family and friends. The real extent of his knowledge of Fitz-Gerald affairs is also unclear; he kept newspaper clippings and collected photographs; he may himself have supplied certain information to Canadian and American newspapers concerning the sixth Duke. Newspaper reports are an obvious source for the impostor, as is memorabilia like the scarf with the inscription 'A gift from Princess Mary'. The latter, while convincing his family of his royal connections, may well have been bought in England: Princess Mary was very active in the war and caused several items bearing her name to be distributed to the troops or sold to raise money. By insuring that his stories were not investigated and thwarting any attempts to establish his case during his lifetime, Charlie Tyler bequeathed a legacy to his children which could only cause confusion and distress, both for them and the eighth Duke's family. That his children, confronted with the unpalatable truth that their father had lied, should have found such news impossible to believe and that they should go to inordinate lengths to sustain faith in their father, is the measure of his duplicity.

During the last hundred years the fortunes of the Leinster FitzGeralds have changed dramatically. No longer do they own vast houses and estates in the country which was their home for seven centuries. But the line is secure, far more so than at any other time in the history of the family. Before his death in 1976 the seventh Duke was a great-grandfather in the male line, an event rare enough among noble families to warrant a special note in *Debrett's*.

Epilogue

IN 1971, an Irish-American named James FitzGerald was touring in Ireland with his wife. He happened to stop, arrested by its grandeur, at Kilkea Castle. Although he had been away from his homeland for many years he was anxious to find out what he could about his family. He was not a Leinster FitzGerald. While wandering in the grounds the couple fell into conversation with a man they took to be a gardener, an elderly man with a lean, weather-beaten face. The conversation turned to the former inhabitants of the castle, and the old man obligingly gave them a brief family history. 'And, to be sure,' he wound up, 'didn't one of them run off with Buffalo Bill's circus?'

The FitzGerald Family Tree

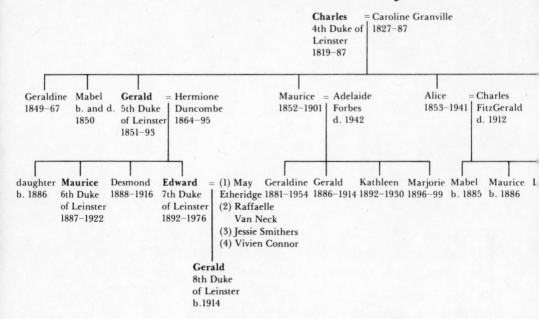

Charles = Caroline Granville
4th Duke of | 1827–87
Leinster
1819–87

Geraldine | Mabel | **Gerald** = Hermione | Maurice = Adelaide | Alice = Charles
1849–67 | b. and d. | 5th Duke | Duncombe | 1852–1901 | Forbes | 1853–1941 | FitzGerald
| 1850 | of Leinster | 1864–95 | | d. 1942 | | d. 1912
| | 1851–93

daughter | **Maurice** | Desmond | **Edward** = (1) May | Geraldine | Gerald | Kathleen | Marjorie | Mabel | Maurice L
b. 1886 | 6th Duke | 1888–1916 | 7th Duke | Etheridge 1881–1954 | 1886–1914 | 1892–1930 | 1896–99 | b. 1885 | b. 1886
| of Leinster | | of Leinster | (2) Raffaelle
| 1887–1922 | | 1892–1976 | Van Neck
| | | | (3) Jessie Smithers
| | | | (4) Vivien Connor

Gerald
8th Duke
of Leinster
b.1914

The Tyler Family Tree

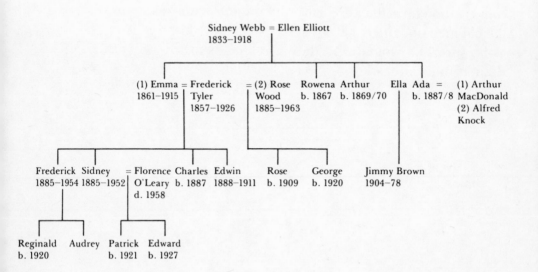

Sidney Webb = Ellen Elliott
1833–1918

(1) Emma = Frederick | = (2) Rose | Rowena | Arthur | Ella Ada = (1) Arthur
1861–1915 | Tyler | Wood | b. 1867 | b. 1869/70 | b. 1887/8 | MacDonald
| 1857–1926 | 1885–1963 | | | (2) Alfred
| | | | | Knock

Frederick | Sidney | = Florence | Charles | Edwin | Rose | George | Jimmy Brown
1885–1954 | 1885–1952 | O'Leary | b. 1887 | 1888–1911 | b. 1909 | b. 1920 | 1904–78
| | d. 1958

Reginald | Audrey | Patrick | Edward
b. 1920 | | b. 1921 | b. 1927

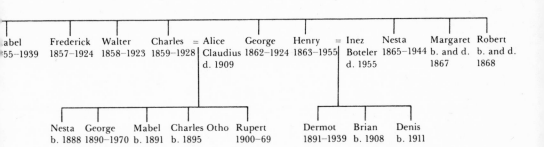

| abel
55–1939 | Frederick
1857–1924 | Walter
1858–1923 | Charles
1859–1928 | = | Alice
Claudius
d. 1909 | George
1862–1924 | Henry
1863–1955 | = | Inez
Boteler
d. 1955 | Nesta
1865–1944 | Margaret
b. and d.
1867 | Robert
b. and d.
1868 |

| Nesta
b. 1888 | George
1890–1970 | Mabel
b. 1891 | Charles Otho
b. 1895 | Rupert
1900–69 | Dermot
1891–1939 | Brian
b. 1908 | Denis
b. 1911 |

The Duncombe Family Tree

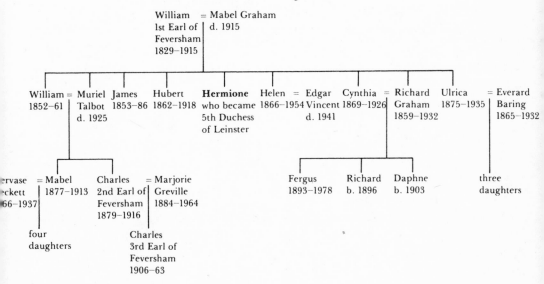

William
1st Earl of
Feversham
1829–1915 = Mabel Graham
d. 1915

| William
1852–61 | = Muriel
Talbot
d. 1925 | James
1853–86 | Hubert
1862–1918 | **Hermione**
who became
5th Duchess
of Leinster | Helen
1866–1954 | = Edgar
Vincent
d. 1941 | Cynthia
1869–1926 | = Richard
Graham
1859–1932 | Ulrica
1875–1935 | = Everard
Baring
1865–1932 |

| ervase
ckett
66–1937 | = Mabel
1877–1913 | Charles
2nd Earl of
Feversham
1879–1916 | = Marjorie
Greville
1884–1964 | Fergus
1893–1978 | Richard
b. 1896 | Daphne
b. 1903 | three
daughters |

four
daughters

Charles
3rd Earl of
Feversham
1906–63

INDEX